KiddiWalks
IN CUMBRIA
& THE LAKE DISTRICT
Chris Bagshaw

COUNTRYSIDE BOOKS
NEWBURY BERKSHIRE

COUNTRYSIDE BOOKS
3 Catherine Road
Newbury, Berkshire

To view our complete range of books,
please visit us at
www.countrysidebooks.co.uk

ISBN 978 1 84674 237 8

Cover design by Jan Marshall
Cover picture © Yuriy Brykaylo/Dreamstime.com

Designed by Peter Davies, Nautilus Design
Produced through MRM Associates Ltd., Reading
Typeset by CJWT Solutions, St Helens
Printed by Information Press, Oxford

Contents

AREA MAP SHOWING THE LOCATIONS OF THE WALKS

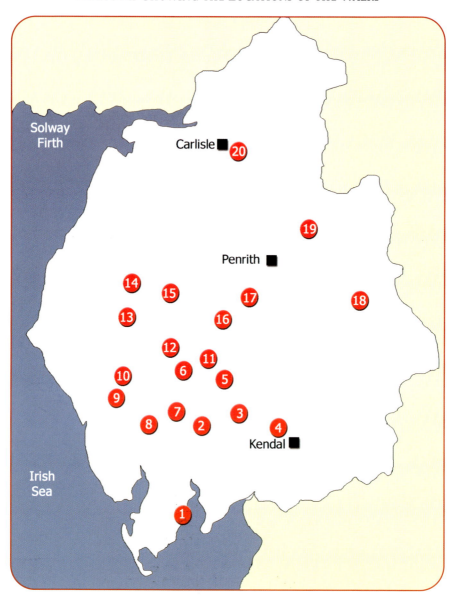

Contents

PUBLISHER'S NOTE

We hope that you obtain considerable enjoyment from this book; great care has been taken in its preparation. Although at the time of publication all routes followed public rights of way or permitted paths, diversion orders can be made and permissions withdrawn.

We cannot, of course, be held responsible for such diversion orders and any inaccuracies in the text which result from these or any other changes to the routes, nor any damage which might result from walkers trespassing on private property. We are anxious though that all details covering the walks are kept up to date and would therefore welcome information from readers which would be relevant to future editions.

The simple sketch maps that accompany the walks in this book are based on notes made by the author whilst checking out the routes on the ground. They are designed to show you how to reach the start, to point out the main features of the overall circuit and they contain a progression of numbers that relate to the paragraphs of the text.

However, for the benefit of a proper map, we do recommend that you purchase the relevant Ordnance Survey sheet covering your walk. The Ordnance Survey maps are widely available, especially through booksellers and local newsagents.

Introduction

At some stage, every parent who loves the outdoors will try and introduce their children to the experience. At times it can be disheartening, and knowing when to cut your losses is a useful skill – this is supposed to be fun remember! But when you *do* get the little ones dressed and ready for action, where should you go? The Lake District is famous for its fine mountains and idyllic valleys, but landscapes don't cut much mustard with a five year old ... so I have chosen a wide range of walks in this book to suit children of different ages. Some are very short and include the important standby of a good play area nearby. They act as a great incentive, I have found. A walk around the Carlisle parks fits this bill, or along the banks of the River Eden at Appleby; Ambleside, Kendal and Keswick can also be relied on to offer active rewards for children who go the distance. But Cumbria, and the Lake District in particular, is not really a place to come for artificial activity aids, so some of these walks have to work a bit harder to keep a child's interest. Giggle Alley in Eskdale Green is a good example: once you have discovered the lost Japanese Garden, you still have the Ravenglass and Eskdale Railway up your sleeve for later in the walk. I have to admit a bias here. I was married in Gatehouse, Eskdale Green, and this walk is effectively a circuit of that beautiful estate. But I was only seven when I fell in love with Eskdale, so the attraction can't all be from my adult self.

Introducing children to walking in the Lake District should also involve a summit or two, perhaps in the hallowed footsteps of Alfred Wainwright. Hallin Fell is my choice for an introduction to fell walking. You get the same sense of outdoors and exhilarating height you would expect, but your car does the donkey work as the walk starts from the top of the Hause in Martindale. The Coniston walk makes similar use of vehicular access to the fells, and though it doesn't reach any summits, it does give you a feel for the village's famous mountain backdrop.

There's no magic formula for walking with children, but judicious use of Polo mints and some of the finest scenery in Britain should help you introduce your little ones to the outdoors with much enjoyment all round.

Chris Bagshaw

1

Bardsea and Sea Wood

From the Beach to the Tangled Wood

Birkrigg Common's stone circle

S tarting along the beach south of Bardsea, which at high tide feels like proper seaside, this is a walk of three distinct parts. First you climb up to the open moorland and limestone of Birkrigg Common, with unfolding views across the bay to the Lancashire coast and the Forest of Bowland beyond. Here you'll find a mysterious stone circle amongst the other prehistoric remains on the moor. Part two takes you into the tangled woodlands of Sea Wood – a semi ancient domain now preserved by the Woodland Trust. And last you get back to the beach. Not all that sandy, is it? But there's usually ice-cream and always a vast open space to run around, make dams, perhaps get a bit muddy, and generally have fun.

Kiddiwalks in Cumbria & the Lake District

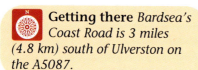

 Getting there *Bardsea's Coast Road is 3 miles (4.8 km) south of Ulverston on the A5087.*

Length of walk 2 miles (3.2 km).
Time 1 hour.
Terrain Beach, woodland and open moor. Not suitable for pushchairs.
Start/Parking Lay-by on Coast Road (GR: SD299740). There are toilets nearby.

Map OS Explorer OL7 The English Lakes (South-eastern area).

Refreshments About 400 yds (366 m) north along Coast Road you'll find a cabin selling hot snacks, sandwiches and ice-creams – open most days. There's also usually an ice-cream van selling locally-made products in one of the parking areas.

◆ Fun Things to See and Do ◆

Well, there are beaches, and there are beaches. This may not be the best beach ever, but there is some sand and a very open space – ideal for **flying kites** – and every so often the sea makes a dramatic appearance. It's a good place for collecting driftwood.

As you walk up the hill you'll see a couple of **unusual towers**, one close by, the other further away. The close-by one is the Bardsea Monument, commemorating the lives of several local figures. The further away one is Ulverston's famous 'lighthouse without a light'. It was built to honour the sailor and explorer Sir John Barrow in 1850. It's modelled on the Eddystone Lighthouse in Devon and was meant to help ships navigate in the bay, though it has never actually been provided with a light.

On Birkrigg Common, see who can find the **stone circle** first. It's hidden in the bracken in summer and there are dozens of tracks in all directions to confuse you.

Sea Wood offers lots of opportunities for games of **hide and seek**.

The Walk

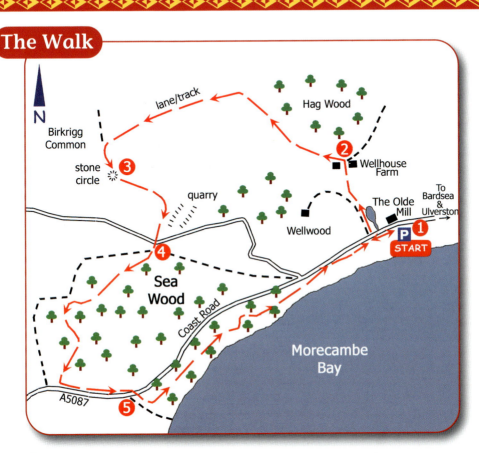

1 From the beachside parking area opposite the Loft Gallery, walk along the footway for 50 yds (46 m) until you're opposite the entrance to Wellwood. Cross the road with care and go through the stile next to the elaborate entrance gate. Keep to the right of the access road between the pond and the fence. The pond served the former mill, which is the white building by the roadside.

Reaching a gate in the access road fence, bear off right across the field, heading for a gap in the hedgerow. Beyond this you'll find a squeeze stile pressing you through the gap between Wellhouse and Wellhouse Farm, leading out to a quiet lane.

2 Turn left, past a cottage and up the enclosed trackway. The wood on the right, known as

9 ◆

Looking across Morecambe Bay from Bardsea

Hag Wood, has been coppiced. As the wood disappears on the right, the track veers left and you get a glimpse of Bardsea Monument. At the top of the track go through a metal gate and out onto the common. Ignore the path right, but now you must locate the stone circle in the midst of the bracken. From the gate, walk ahead 50 paces, then turn left and walk a similar distance. That should get you to the centre of the circle, or at least somewhere near!

3 Imagine the stone circle is a roundabout and you came in at one point; now take the second left and descend with a wall on your left. It's roughly south-south-east and should lead you to a wall corner. Keep to the left-hand path for another 50 yds (46 m)

and you'll reach the edge of some shallow quarry workings. Bear right, across the head of the quarry to reach a minor road.

4 Cross over and locate a gate in the wall opposite, leading into Sea Wood. Follow the path into the wood, keeping right when you have the choice. The path descends eventually to a gate leading out onto the main road. Turn left, crossing a lay-by then staying on the wide verge before crossing over with care at the point where the woods appear on the opposite side of the road.

5 Here you'll find a path that ducks down the side of the wood, but shortly offers you a turning to the left. Take this and follow the meandering woodland trail all the way to the end of the wood by the beach at some large boulders. Keep ahead, choosing the right-hand side of the hedgerow ahead and a beachside track leading all the way back to your parking area.

◆ Background Notes ◆

Birkrigg Common opens out at the top of the walk, a small quarry betraying its underlying limestone. The stone circle may date from the Bronze Age, between 1700 and 1400 BC. It was known locally as the Druid's Temple though there's no evidence of druidical use. The remains of five cremated humans were discovered in 1911 in the centre of the circle.

Another prominent feature seen from up on the common is **Chapel Island** out in the bay, towards the Leven estuary. This once held a chapel related to Conishead Priory, on the facing shore. It was built by the Cistercian monks to serve fishermen and travellers across the sands. Nothing remains of the original structure but in the 1820s, Colonel Bradyll of Conishead added a romantic ruin to enhance the view from his new house on the site of the original priory.

Sea Wood is the centrepiece of this walk. Unusual in the context of Morecambe Bay – there aren't many shoreline woods between the Solway and North Wales – it is owned and managed by the Woodland Trust. It's classified as semi ancient natural woodland, which means it hasn't been too interfered with, possibly since as far back as the 16th century when it was owned by Lady Jane Grey, who was very briefly Queen of England in 1553. It became Crown property soon after that, and was acquired by Lancashire County Council in the 1950s. If it looks a bit untidy inside, that's because the woodland management plan has allowed for many fallen trees and branches to stay in situ. This is great for biodiversity but lends a slightly unkempt appearance to the woods. Up until the 1930s there were charcoal burners operating in the woods, coppicing sections of new growth to supply their ovens. Timber from Sea Wood was also floated along the shore to Ulverston for use in shipbuilding.

Grizedale Forest

What's That in the Trees?

The ultra modern Yan Building at Grizedale

Grizedale Forest is the biggest area of woodland in the Lake District. It's not just about trees though. Since the 1960s the Forestry Commission has allowed the forest to become a huge sculpture park, with all manner of surprising installations hidden in its depths. On this short walk you'll spy a few of these and maybe a few of the other woodland residents. Roe deer are frequently spotted nibbling at the grass and younger trees, and squirrels, badgers and foxes all call this place home. To help you find your way in the woods this walk is waymarked by purple-topped posts. The described route is the shorter of the two Bogle Crag Trails, but the longer version can be done fairly easily instead if you have more time available or your party is a little quicker on its feet. It's a good idea to get a copy of the trail map from the shop in the Courtyard at the main Grizedale visitor centre before you start.

Getting there *The Bogle Crag pay & display car park is about a mile (1.6 km) south of the Grizedale Forest visitor centre. This in turn is on a minor road about 3 miles (4.8 km) south of Hawkshead.*

Length of walk 2½ miles (4 km).
Time 1½ hours.
Terrain Forest tracks and paths, some quite steep. Not suitable for pushchairs.
Start/Parking Bogle Crag car park (GR: SD338933). Toilets at the visitor centre.
Map OS Explorer OL7 The English Lakes (South-eastern area); Forestry Commission Grizedale Forest trail map (available from Grizedale Forest visitor centre).
Refreshments The Café in the Forest is in the Courtyard at the Grizedale Forest visitor centre. It serves a good range from light snacks to more substantial meals, with a children's menu also available.

◆ Background Notes ◆

It's well worth stopping at the visitor centre shop before you drive on to the Bogle Crag car park. As well as the trail map and the tree guide, you'll find a guide to the sculptures. The numbers in the guide correspond with those on the trail map, though in truth it doesn't offer you much further explanation – you have to use your imagination if you're considering meaning or purpose. A few of the sculptures are a little way off the trail, so some searching might be necessary. That's when the reference guide helps most, so you know what you're looking for. There are over 60 sculptures in the forest, with perhaps the best known being around the visitor centre itself.

Grizedale Forest covers over 6,000 acres (2,428 ha) and includes areas of woodland that were planted for commercial use over 200 years ago. The Forestry Commission took over the forest in 1937, establishing its headquarters at Grizedale Hall. The hall was demolished in 1957 and nothing remains of the old building now except the grand terrace that you see beside the ultra modern Yan building at the top of the visitor centre car park.

The Walk

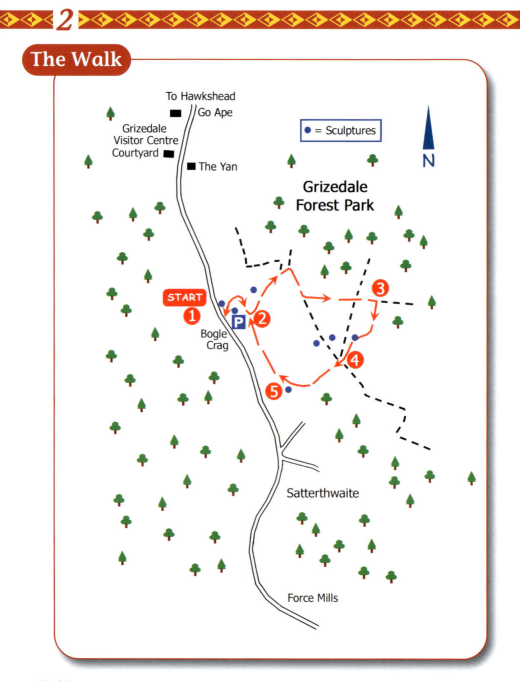

To Hawkshead
Go Ape
Grizedale
Visitor Centre
Courtyard
The Yan

● = Sculptures

N

Grizedale
Forest Park

START
1
P
2
Bogle
Crag
3
4
5

Satterthwaite

Force Mills

1 From the car park walk up past the barrier into the woods, following the purple marked trail. Charles Bray's 'Light Column' is to your left and Belle Shafir's 'The Seer's Well' is the striking arrangement to your right.

2 As the path swings round to the right stay on the forest road, which now swings left, continuing to climb. Take the right-hand fork at the next junction and in 50 paces or so go right again. As you round a bend, a marker invites you to go left up a rougher track into an area of thinned woodland. A short pull levels out into a much younger plantation where the right-hand path allows you to avoid a particularly wet section. The paths merge again and you should find yourself at a crossroads in almost open moorland. Keep straight ahead with the purple marker on a narrowing path, still heading gently uphill.

Who's that climbing the rope?

3 Towards the top of the rise, pass through the deer fence and go right with the signpost for the Bogle Crag short route. The path opens out at Jony Easterby's 'Wind Thrust' installation before descending to a forest road in a clearfelled area.

4 There are two more installations off to the right here, marked on prominent rocks, though they are not easy to locate. Stay with the purple markers to cross the forest road, descending a rib of higher ground before dropping more steeply back into the forest. The path swings right, over a wall, then descends more gently and

Robert Bryce Muir's 'Mea Culpa' comes into view down to your left.

5 Stay with this contouring path, passing the end of the longer route, which joins from the left, and a circular pit installation. Eventually you reach a junction with your outward route. Turn left and follow the forest road back to the start. The tall tree on the final bend has a tiny carving of a figure on it.

◆ Fun Things to See and Do ◆

There are **seven peculiar sculptures** hidden in the forest on this walk. See if you can find them all. Not all of them are exactly on the route so you'll have to look at the trail map to locate them. The most peculiar is called 'Mea Culpa'. You'll find it near the end of the walk. The two men seem to be working very hard. When you get closer you'll see their muscles are made of thin strips of metal. Near the start and finish of the walk, one big tree has a carving of a little man on it – can you find it?

There will be plenty of **animal tracks** to spot as you go round. It's easy to pick out the footprints of people and their dogs, but see if you can identify any others. Deer footprints are often particularly clear, but they also look a bit like sheep hoofmarks.

On a forest walk it's important to be able to tell the wood from the **trees**. The visitor centre shop has a handy leaflet that will help you identify all the different species – it's not just Christmas trees and oaks here.

3

Bowness-on-Windermere

Scrambling on the Crags

The view from Biskey Howe

Most people who visit the Lake District end up in Bowness-on-Windermere at some stage – it's the lively lakeside town with the pubs and clubs, the promenades and the boat rides, and for children there are some good parks, the Beatrix Potter Museum and the boats are fun. But step away from the crowded streets for a while and a whole new world opens up. This walk explores the hill country above the town – never too far away, but far enough to feel more like the Lake District and less like Blackpool. What's always surprising is how easily the town is lost, even from the enticing craggy heights of Biskey Howe, barely a stone's throw from the centre. Post Knott is the other set-piece viewpoint visited, along with an inviting section of the Dales Way.

3

Getting there *Bowness-on-Windermere is on the junction of the A592 and the A5074 about a mile or so south of Windermere town.*

Length of walk 2 miles (3.2 km).
Time 1 hour.
Terrain Town streets, woods and farmland overlooking the lake. Not suitable for pushchairs.

Start/Parking The pay-and-display car park on Rayrigg Road, which is the A592 (GR: SD402970). There are toilets here.
Map OS Explorer OL7 The English Lakes (South-eastern area).
Refreshments There are so many options in Bowness you may well be spoiled for choice.

The Walk

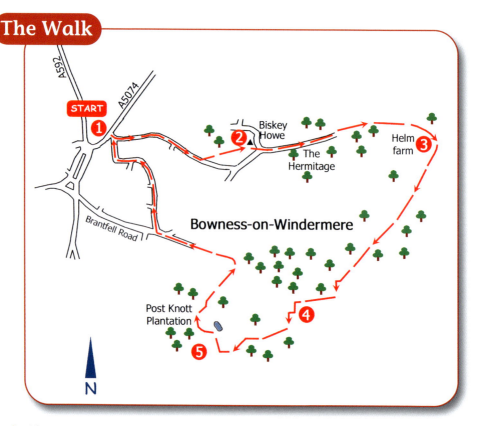

1 In the centre of Bowness, find the mini-roundabout that marks the junction of the A592, Rayrigg Road, and the A5074, Crag Brow. Walk up Crag Brow, heading towards the Edinburgh Woollen Mill and the World of Beatrix Potter shops. Turn right here, up Helm Road, ascending steadily past the Windermere Hydro Hotel. As the road narrows and the pavement vanishes, take a path on the left up into some woods. The path rises steeply, emerging at the surprisingly lovely viewpoint of Biskey Howe.

2 When you've had your fill of the view and scrambling on the crags, leave the viewpoint by the path at the back between the rocks and descend to rejoin the road at the bottom of some steps. Turn right and then quickly left with a footpath sign up a

◆ Fun Things to See and Do ◆

It's always difficult to tear yourself away from the Beatrix Potter shops and the like, but there's a lot of fun to be had on this walk. The first object is **Biskey Howe**, a bite size chunk of rock in the middle of what feels like someone's back garden. It's great for a scramble and the views are surprising. Where did the town go?

Look for the ancient **datestone on Helm Farm**. Not everything in Bowness is Victorian!

When you reach **Post Knott** you get another chance to look out across Windermere lake. How many of the hills on the horizon can you name?

There's a **children's play area** on Langrigg Drive, towards the end of the walk.

At the end of the walk, you could drive northwards to the National Park's main **visitor centre at Brockhole**, a few miles up the lake. Now that is a playground and a half ...

driveway towards Helm Farm. Ignore the Permissive Path to Post Knott and continue on the driveway surrounded by rhododendrons. At the next junction, maintain your direction towards Helm Farm, enjoying the unusual 'Toyland' quality of some of the houses you pass on the way. Stay with the footpath signs as they direct you around the back of some houses, between the gate lodges. Eventually you emerge behind Helm Farm.

3 Follow the track round the farm cottage and round the corner go through a tiny gate and cross a field, heading for a signpost on the wall corner ahead. From here, an obvious line leads you to a gate in a wall. Beyond this, cross a surprising area of open parkland. Ignore driveways to left and right but keep ahead, following a yellow footpath sign. Go through a kissing gate and head for another gateway in the wall ahead. Maintain your direction across the next field, to a kissing gate and an intersecting path.

4 This is the Dales Way; turn right, through a kissing gate to another path junction. Go

straight across, ignoring turnings to a gate into another field. Turn left, up the steps and follow the path as it swirls up the hill before crossing a stile at the top. The summit of Brant Fell can be reached by turning left here. We turn right, over one stile, then another to join a narrow, muddy path between the forest fence and a wall. As you duck through the holly another stile leads onto access land, where a leafy path leads out to the unfolding view of Post Knott.

5 From the summit, looking towards the lake bear right down the hill, through a kissing gate into the woods. In the woods, bear left, keeping on the downward track, maintaining your direction where it levels out. At a four-way signpost, turn left with the Dales Way, down the hill towards Bowness. As you descend look out for the sign 'Ilkley 81 miles'. Through the gate at the bottom of the field join a steeply descending road, carrying straight on to reach the centre of Bowness or turning right, along Langrigg Drive, to return to Helm Road. There is a small play area about 200 yds (183 m) along here on the left.

◆ Background Notes ◆

Bowness-on-Windermere (it gets the suffix to distinguish it from Bowness-on-Solway) is the original part of the settlement that sprawls down to the lake from Windermere railway station. The two communities are virtually joined into one now, but until the arrival of the railway in 1847 the one higher up the hill was just a hamlet known as Birthwaite. Shrewd marketing led the developers to name it Windermere, and left the rest of us to forever bracket the word 'town' after it to distinguish it from the lake.

Old Bowness developed as a fishing village in the sheltered bay facing Belle Isle. The church of St Martin is probably the oldest building remaining. It was rebuilt in 1483 to replace a previous building, which burned down. The streets around St Martin's retain an olde-worlde feel quite distinct from the Victorian resort buildings that abound further up the hill. The Windermere Hydro Hotel is a good example of the latter; dating from the end of the 19th century, when taking a hydropathic cure was very popular, it exudes a majestic sense of importance. Today it is reinvented as a modern spa hotel.

Above the Hydro is **Biskey Howe**, one of several viewpoints across Windermere and probably the most accessible. The lake stretches away to the north, with the Langdales and Loughrigg Fell framing the horizon. Across the lake, the view is bounded by Claife Heights.

Helm Farm – now holiday accommodation – has some features dating back to 1691. This is quite early by Lakeland standards. The area was not blessed with sufficient peace and wealth to leave too many domestic buildings from before this time.

Post Knott is another classic viewing spot, this time with a panorama of Ferry Nab and the lower lake to consider. Again it is remarkable how the town below doesn't intrude into your view. The Victorians created an easy trackway up to the Knott connecting all the way to the Helm Farm road we came out on. But that would be for a different walk …

4

Around Kendal Castle

A Queen's Childhood Home

The north-west tower of Kendal Castle

This isn't a country walk. You are likely to meet lots of other people, exercising dogs, skateboarding, gardening, cycling, or some may just be walking to or from work. But in return for this comparative busy-ness, you get a brilliant castle, with towers to climb and cellars to explore; you get to walk in the course of an old canal; and might even get to watch some snowboarders cutting some air in a half pipe, even in summer (really!). If that isn't enough to excite you, there's a children's play area near the start of the walk and if you feel like extending the walk by a few hundred yards you can have a look at one of Cumbria's best museums, or even go shopping in the centre of town.

Getting there *The car park is next to Kendal United's community rooms on Castle Drive. This is best approached from Parkside Road, which connects the A684 by the Castle Green Hotel with the A65, Lound Road, on the south side of Kendal.*

Length of walk 2 miles (3.2 km).
Time 1 hour.
Terrain Parkland paths, pavement and grass. Just about suitable for a pushchair (there are some steps).
Start/Parking Castle Drive free car park (GR: SD524924).
Map OS Explorer OL7 The English Lakes (South-eastern area).
Refreshments Your best bet is to cross the river at the bottom of Sunnyside/Parr Street halfway through the walk and head for the café at the Abbott Hall Gallery. If that's not your cup of tea, there are plenty more choices in town.

◆ Fun Things to See and Do ◆

The **castle** is a perfect place to explore. You can climb to the top of the north-west tower, discover the cellars and the castle's deep well and investigate the moat. Can you find the medieval toilet? It was known as a garderobe and it's in the north-west tower. Waste from here fell through a hole into the moat.

As well as the ruins, this is one **big grassy hill**. It's great for rolling, cartwheeling or just flying a kite.

A short distance into the walk is a little grove of trees. Look for the benches with the unusual leaf motifs. Beyond this you skirt round the cemetery and the allotments. How many **different types of vegetable** can you see growing?

The middle of the walk passes the top of the **dry ski slope**. In the evening it's fun to watch the snowboarders pretending they are in the Alps.

The Walk

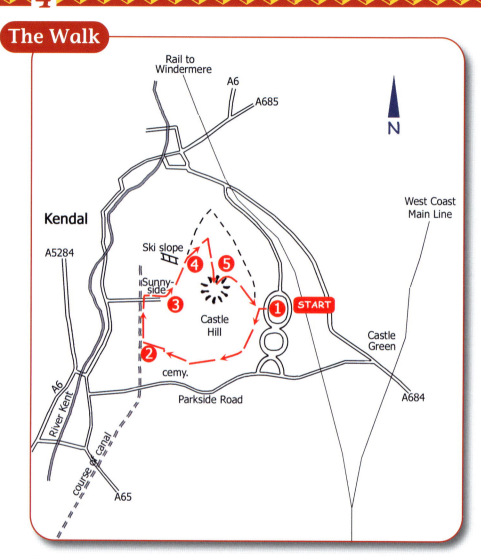

1 From the car park, don't go through the gate into the castle park, but pick out an enclosed path between the football field and the castle park boundary.

Shortly, on the left, you'll find a set of benches with leaf motifs, the BMX track and the cricket ground. Keeping to the foot of the castle mound, continue on a

The canal bridge at point 2 of the walk

gravel path. You'll soon come to the cemetery on your left. Swing right with the wall on your left and walk down the hill. The track descends more steeply through an opening and down a slope by the allotments. Join a concrete path into the woods and then on the level beside the allotments. When you come to a junction of tracks, go straight ahead towards some steps and a crossing path.

2 This is the route of the Lancaster Canal. Turn right along the line of the canal to reach a bridge. Go under this and in a few paces turn left, going back on yourself, to ascend the ramp up on to the street. Turn left along the pavement and walk up the street known as Sunnyside.

3 Go through the iron gates at the top and turn left into the woods. An obvious path follows the line of the wall on the left, finally ending at a crossing flight of steps above the dry ski slope. Ascend the steps and at the top a red arrow points you left across the top of the ski slope.

4 The track rises up into a green field. Coming out of the trees, you get to see the castle and a great view out of town. Cut across the grass to intersect a wide track and turn right, up the hill to the castle. There is plenty to see at the castle and a tower to climb. Note there is no way out of the castle courtyard except through the main entrance over the moat.

5 When you've finished, return

to the entrance and with your back to the castle, bear left on a path that follows the line of the moat. Circle the castle almost completely before picking out a track down to the right, across the grassy slope to the gate and the car park at the start of the walk.

◆ Background Notes ◆

This is **Kendal's second castle**. You can see the first attempt from the top of the hill. It's on the other side of the valley and it's marked by an obelisk. The new castle was built on this high glacial drumlin (ridge) towards the end of the 12th century. There are plenty of diagrams on the site depicting how it used to look and what the various bits of ruined masonry represent. The castle's most famous occupant was Katherine Parr, who was born here in 1512. In a relatively short life she managed to pack in four husbands, one of whom happened to be King Henry VIII (born 1491, reigned 1509–1547). Katherine was Henry's sixth wife and she outlived him by a year. She died in childbirth in 1548 having already married again, this time Thomas Seymour of Sudeley. For a short period in 1544 Katherine ruled England as Regent, whilst her husband was away fighting the French. The castle site is now cared for by South Lakeland District Council and is accessible at all times.

At the bottom of the allotments you join the course of the **Lancaster Canal**. Completed in 1819 it connected the town to Preston, 50 miles to the south, where it joined the rest of the English canal network. The canal carried its last commercial load in 1947 and was drained in the mid 1950s following a leak near Stainton. The Kendal end was filled in and the course as far as Tewitfield (just south of the Cumbria border) was breached in several places by road schemes, notably the M6. There are plans to restore the canal but as yet they have not resulted in much demonstrable action.

Kendal Ski Club's dry slope was originally established in 1984 and is run by volunteers. Lessons and freestyle sessions are available to non-members, visit www.kendalski.co.uk for details.

5

Ambleside and the Sweden Bridges

Twice across the Beck

High Sweden Bridge

This is a fairly easy walk, though the outward climb may need lots of encouragement for little feet. Your efforts are continually rewarded, however, by some breathtaking views unfolding over Windermere. There's also a series of little wayside craggy outcrops that are asking to be scaled by energetic would-be Boningtons, not to mention their suitability for pleasant picnic spots. The higher of the two bridges is a perfectly formed packhorse bridge over Scandale Beck and on the far side you'll find another idyllic spot for a picnic, though this time the crags fall precipitously towards the beck so a little care should be exercised. The return leg takes you through quiet woodlands on a rough but broad track, finally leading you back into busy Ambleside at the foot of the famous 'Struggle' up the Kirkstone Pass.

5

 Getting there *Ambleside is at the northern end of Windermere on the A591. The main car parks for this walk are at the north end of the town on Rydal Road.*

Length of walk 3 miles (4.8 km).
Time 2 hours.
Terrain Town streets, then open fell and wooded valley. Not suitable for pushchairs.
Start/Parking Pay-and-display car parks off Rydal Road (GR: NY375047).

◆ Fun Things to See and Do ◆

As you start the walk, look for the '**house on the bridge**' (Bridge House). It's one of Ambleside's most famous sights and is over 300 years old. It was probably built as a summer house, or as an apple store for the owner of Ambleside Hall. These days it is a very tiny information centre for the National Trust.

There are some interesting **trees and crags to clamber on** while doing the steady climb up to High Sweden Bridge – nice views too!

High Sweden Bridge is a bit like the bridge with the house on it, only without the house. It is a packhorse bridge – there are no sides because these would have got in the way of the packs on either flank of the horses.

On the way down keep an eye open for the **dank cave**. It's an old quarry working that looks as if it might conceal a troll or two.

In Ambleside itself it's worth visiting **the park** beyond the main car park. There's a play area, as well as lots of open space and funny little rocky clumps to climb over. The main entrance is on Vicarage Road. It's also worth looking in on the **Armitt Collection and Ambleside Museum** (open Monday to Saturday; entrance fee), which has some original Beatrix Potter drawings among other interesting exhibits.

Ambleside and the Sweden Bridges

Map OS Explorer OL7 The English Lakes (South-eastern area).
Refreshments The centre of Ambleside is awash with opportunities. Lucy's on a Plate in Church Street is always popular with families but there are many other choices.

The Walk

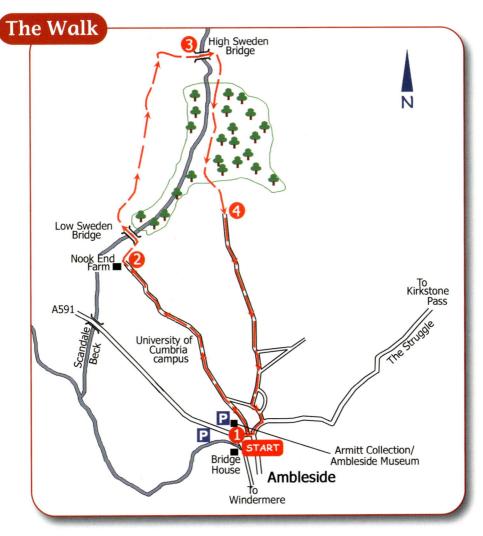

High Sweden Bridge

N

Low Sweden Bridge

Nook End Farm

A591

Scandale Beck

University of Cumbria campus

To Kirkstone Pass

The Struggle

P

P

START

Bridge House

Ambleside

To Windermere

Armitt Collection/ Ambleside Museum

Kiddiwalks in Cumbria & the Lake District

5

1 Head for the mini-roundabout on the Grasmere road, at the foot of the 'Struggle'. Turn up the hill signposted towards Kirkstone (be careful here as there isn't much of a pavement). Turn left almost immediately, along Nook Lane. Keep straight ahead now on the enclosed lane, passing the old Charlotte Mason College campus on the left. Continue on the lane until you reach a farmyard and the road end.

2 Go through the yard, picking out a descending track on the far side beyond a gate. Follow this down to a bridge. This is Low Sweden Bridge. Cross it and follow the track beyond as it swings round to the right and begins a gradual ascent. Through a gateway, the track swings half left and continues up the hill. Plodding on, see how many lakes you can spot. Passing through a gap in the wall you'll be pleased to know that over half the climbing is done now. Beyond the gap, keep going gently uphill, passing several idyllic picnic spots near some enticingly scrambly-looking rocks. At last the way ahead levels out and beyond the next wall gap a small yellow arrow points right, passing tarnlets and bogs to a ladder stile. Cross the stile and continue downwards to a tiny bridge over the beck.

3 Cross the bridge and turn right, passing some exciting waterfalls, then keeping right as you join a larger track descending into the woods. The path continues gently downhill to a gate and onwards, passing some old quarry workings on the left. Through another gate, the track becomes a narrow lane. Curving away from the woods and the waterfalls into more open country, the lane twists and turns, passing a peculiar tower on the left. Beyond this, a gate leads out to a surfaced road.

4 Continue down the hill, keeping on the downward turn when you have the option. There's very little traffic on this road, but do take care. Joining a busier road (Smithy Brow) turn right, descending past the Golden Rule to the foot of the 'Struggle' road and the mini-roundabout, from where you can return to your car.

Ambleside and the Sweden Bridges

◆ Background Notes ◆

Disappointingly no actual Swedes were involved in the two eponymous bridges, though the people who named them were using some Scandinavian terms. **High and Low Sweden bridges** take their name from an Old Norse word for an area cleared by burning. Likewise Scandale Beck means the 'short valley' in Lakeland dialect. So much of the local language derives from Old Norse that you could be forgiven for thinking this was some sort of Viking enclave. The reality may be that Norse settlers came here from Ireland in the 9th century and mixed with the local Britons and even a few English to create a rich hybrid language and culture, much of which lingers in place names and local customs today.

The start of the walk passes the extensive campus buildings of the old **Charlotte Mason teacher training college**. Mason was one of those formidable Victorian women who set out to 'get things done'. She pioneered an approach to children's education that began with the assumption that children were 'born persons', and developed from their practical experiences. She established the college in Ambleside in 1892 as the House of Education and it became a byword for innovative teacher training, especially including aspects of outdoor education. In the way of these things, the college merged with Lancaster University in 1992, then in 1996 was hived off to St Martin's College, which in turn was swallowed up by the new University of Cumbria in 2007. The new institution was straightaway hurled into a financial maelstrom and at the time of writing the whole campus had been mothballed pending a decision on its future use. In such a beautiful and prominent location it is to be hoped that some sensible outcome is achieved.

Ambleside grew as a tourist town in the 19th century despite the fact that the railway never reached it. It wasn't through want of trying – the initial cutting can still be traced leaving Windermere station. But with Wordsworth et al opposed (the poet was official 'Distributor of Stamps' in Westmorland and had an office on Church Street), the development ran out of steam.

6

Along Great Langdale

Woods, Quarries and a Fairy Castle

The village of Chapel Stile

This fairly easy walk weaves amidst trees and old quarry workings and at one stage there is a glimpse of a fairy castle, high up on the hillside out of reach. Great Langdale is at the heart of the real Lake District; where the hills become steeper and pointier, and the walking becomes a little bit rougher. But neither the shorter nor the longer of these circular routes worries too much about hills. For the most part they explore the broad valley bottom of the larger of the two Langdales, from charming Elterwater along quiet lanes through quiet woods to ancient farms. But not everything is peace and tranquillity. You'll occasionally hear the rumble of slate quarry traffic from the well-screened workings at Yew Crags and, as you pass the upmarket holiday lodges of the Langdale Estate, you'll be looking over the site of an old gunpowder factory – they used to test the finished product by firing a huge canon from beside the modern bowling green across the fields into Elter Water itself.

Along Great Langdale

Getting there *Elterwater is 4 miles (6.4 km) west of Ambleside on the B5343. Turn left into the village to find the Britannia Inn, car parks and toilets.*

Length of walk 3½ miles (5.6 km); shorter route 2 miles (3.2 km).
Time 2 hours for the longer route.
Terrain Quiet lanes, field paths and tracks. The shorter route could be done with an all-terrain pushchair, but pushing would be harder going on the longer circuit.
Start/Parking The National Trust pay-and-display car park in the centre of Elterwater (GR: NY327047). There are toilets here.
Map OS Explorer OL7 The English Lakes (South-eastern area).
Refreshments The Britannia Inn

◆ Fun Things to See and Do ◆

The start of the walk is along a surfaced road, but there are some interesting things to spy on either side. Can you spot the **cave entrance**, the **red deer antlers** or the **hidden quarry**? Beyond Baysbrown, there's a **fairy castle** up on the fellside. It's known as the Oak Howe Needle and it's actually a section of cliff from the adjacent crags.

In the village of Chapel Stile, everything is made of **slate**. Can you find any interesting pieces? Some look like animals or space ships, others look as if they will be really good for skimming in the river. Even the village swings are slate related, being next to an old crane from the quarry.

There are more **holes in the ground** to spot on the way back, but none you can actually go in. To find some more friendly holes to explore, you'll have to drive round to Little Langdale from Elterwater, and walk across the valley from the Three Shires Inn. Here you'll find the famous **Cathedral Quarry** complex. You'll need a torch and should obey the warning signs.

6

The Walk

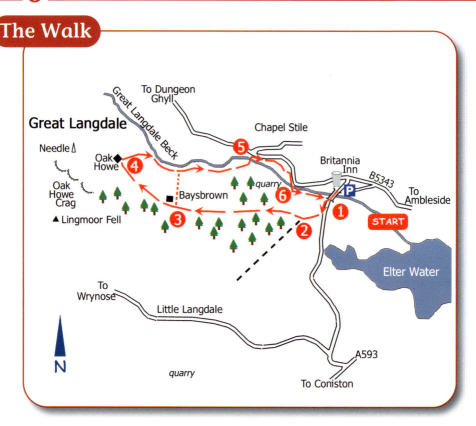

has a lovely outdoor seating area in the centre of the village and serves excellent locally-sourced food and beer. There's a good children's menu too. The Brambles Tearoom and the Wainwright's Inn at Chapel Stile are passed on the route.

1 Turn left out of the main National Trust car park and cross the bridge over Great Langdale Beck. Walk up the lane past the Youth Hostel and then take the right turn up a surfaced lane, signposted as a challenging option to Coniston for cyclists.

2 As the lane ahead steepens, take the right turn to pass a cottage with antlers over the door. Continue on this lane as it passes through woodland riddled with old quarry workings. In ¾ mile (1.2 km) it emerges in farmland at Baysbrown and the lane ends.

3 You can cut the walk short here by turning right, across the fields, to meet the route again beside Great Langdale Beck, but for the longer walk, go through the farmyard, bearing slightly left on the far side to join a bridleway. Ignore the quarry access road leading up to the right and stay with the signposted bridleway, shortly directed by an incongruous road sign to Great Langdale and Dungeon Ghyll, clearly lifted from somewhere else. The track continues through woodland before emerging in open fell and descending to Oak Howe.

4 You'll see the Oak Howe Needle on the horizon up to your left here. Head to the right of the farmhouse, walking out into the valley bottom to a bridge. Don't cross the bridge, but veer right to join the riverside path through the flat fields and eventually meet the short route down from Baysbrown at a campsite. Continue for a few hundred yards to New Bridge on the left and cross over to the Chapel Stile bank.

5 The path weaves between slate walls to a junction. Turn right up a path signposted to the village centre. Go through a gate

The path at Baysbrown

and pass a pair of swings next to an old quarry crane, emerging on an access road. Maintain your direction at the next junction to continue down a rough track at the back of the schoolhouse. Descend to the main road and turn left to visit Chapel Stile's Co-op and tearoom (though note there are no longer public toilets here), or turn right to continue the walk. Pass the Wainwright's pub and at the far side of its car park, pick out a bridleway sign directing you to a bridge back over the beck.

6 Cross this and turn left along the riverbank beneath the piles of slate waste. After 250 yds (229 m) or so the track rises to join the quarry access road opposite one of its underground workings. Bear left, maintaining your direction and descending to the junction in Elterwater. Turn left over the bridge to return to the car park.

◆ Background Notes ◆

Quarrying has been a way of life in this part of Langdale for over 300 years. The quarries in Elterwater are still working and are currently owned by Burlington. Do watch out for quarry lorries on the last part of the walk and beware of hidden drops if you wander into any of the workings. The **Cathedral Quarry** at Little Langdale is worth a visit to get a glimpse of what the vast scale of the underground quarry faces are like. It's owned by the National Trust and can be explored with care.

The other important industry here was making **gunpowder**. It required charcoal (made from the local woodlands), saltpetre (imported from as far away as India and Chile) and sulphur (imported from Italy). The process also required water power and plenty of space, both of which Elterwater had in abundance. Manufacturing began in 1824 to supply the local quarries and mines, and continued until 1928, when the site was dismantled. The remaining buildings have been incorporated into the Langdale Estate holiday complex that you can see across the river towards the end of the walk.

Farming was Langdale's third major industry, and the valley's agricultural history can be traced back several thousand years. Baysbrown Farm was granted to Conishead Priory in the 13th century, and the medieval ring garth – the wall that separated the fertile valley land from the waste – can still be identified on the fellside above the dale bottom.

Walna Scar and Banishead

In Search of Coniston's Old Men

You could be forgiven for thinking that Coniston was all about the lake, and the towering Old Man, the highest point of a range of mountains that dominates the village. But Coniston has a lot more history than first meets the eye. This walk, which is probably best suited to older children, discovers a hidden valley, a magical waterfall tumbling into a blue/green lagoon and a series of ancient homesteads, possibly dating back over 4,000 years. It finishes on the famous Walna Scar Road – not really a road at all for most of its length, but an impressive path heading up into the mountains, eventually crossing over into the Duddon Valley beyond the skyline. You'll see the lake, and the Old Man from this walk, but you'll also discover some of Coniston's little known secrets.

7

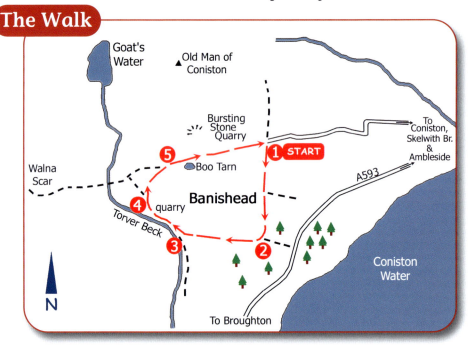

Getting there *Coniston is on the A593. From the centre of the village you need to go seriously uphill. You can take the road signposted toward the Sun Inn, or the next one, which leads up towards the old station. Both lead to the punishingly steep beginnings of the Walna Scar Road. It might be a first gear job some of the way, but the road levels out eventually to a gate. Beyond this you'll find an extensive, but rough, free car park. Don't forget to shut the gate behind you.*

Length of walk 3½ miles (5.6 km).
Time 2 hours.
Terrain Mostly moorland tracks and some old quarry workings. Not suitable for pushchairs and probably best suited to older children. Tracks through the workings are quite substantial but there are some exposed edges so exercise care. The ground can be very wet underfoot, so wellies would be a good idea at most times of the year.
Start/Parking Walna Scar Road, by the fell gate (GR: SD288970).
Map OS Explorer OL6 The

The Walk

Walna Scar and Banishead

English Lakes (South-western area).

Refreshments There is plenty of choice of cafés and pubs in Coniston village at the bottom of the hill.

1 From the car park, return to the fell gate and turn right, following the path beside a stone wall. Passing a ladder stile (don't cross it) you get a good view of the lake and John Ruskin's house at Brantwood on the far shore. Stay with the wall on your left until you meet some sheepfolds, beyond which you'll see a gate in the wall. Go through this and continue ahead with the wall now on your right and descend through a series of boggy dells to a wall corner by a ladder stile.

2 Turn right here, over the stile, and walk up the next pasture, keeping a tumbledown wall to your left. When you meet the corner of a proper wall, an arrow points you to its left, where after a few paces you'll find a difficult stone stile. Traverse this with care and on the far side a path leads you through sheep-cropped turf and bracken down into the valley

◆ Fun Things to See and Do ◆

Look for the Old Men! The mountain is easy to spot – it's the highest point you can see above you – but the other 'old men' are a bit less obvious. Local miners would call anyone who had mined in their area before them 't'owd men'. On this walk you'll find a few places where they have been. Driving up the hill you'll see a cave on the left-hand side. This is an old copper mine.

On the second half of the walk, you'll find a **strange landscape of slate and rubble**, and several more **surprising holes in the ground**. One of these has a whole river coming out of it! A bit higher up you'll see where it comes from – there's a huge crater (be very careful by the edge). A waterfall drops dramatically into one end of a blue green lagoon, and somewhere in the depths unseen, the water flows out again to emerge from the cave you pass.

of Torver Beck. Becoming boggy again towards the bottom, the path veers right slightly to intersect a larger track coming up the valley.

3 Turn right on this, now ascending by the side of the beck towards the piles of quarry spoil ahead. Go through a gate and cross a little wooden footbridge. Aim to the left of the nearest spoil heap and you'll find yourself in a little valley of slate. Continue upwards and at the top of the rise you'll see a branch of the beck spewing out of a massive hole in the ground. As the path levels, a fence ahead prevents you from wandering into the massive hole of Banishead Quarry. It's worth peering in, though, to see the deep lagoon and waterfall, where Torver Beck has breached the quarry wall.

4 Continue upwards on the grassy path to the right of the big hole. The lumps and bumps in the moor to the right here are the remains of a Bronze Age settlement. Soon a right fork comes into view. Take this green stripe across the bracken to meet the Walna Scar Road.

5 Turn right along this famous old track past the access to Bursting Stone Quarry and Boo Tarn to return to the fell gate car park.

◆ Background Notes ◆

Banishead Quarry was operational in the 19th century. It's one of many in this area producing a distinctive olive green slate. The pool, which is nearly 30 ft (10 m) deep is occasionally used by divers. Slate was carted down to the railway station at Torver. **Bursting Stone Quarry**, passed towards the end of the walk, has supplied building projects as far away as Los Angeles.

The moorland known as **The Rigg** has several much older archaeological sites though they are a little indistinct. These are the remains of a settlement dating back to the Bronze Age, roughly 4,000 years ago, when the climate was milder than it is now.

Birks Bridge and Upper Dunnerdale

Who's for a Game of Pooh Ships?

Beautiful Dunnerdale

The upper reaches of Dunnerdale are wild and remote. Beneath Birks Bridge the River Duddon tumbles through a dramatic chasm, but upstream of the bridge it burbles through a landscape of rough pastures, only recently revealed from beneath the cloak of forestry plantations that had hidden it for more than 50 years. The walk follows the riverbank for a few hundred yards before crossing the now wild torrent by an ancient packhorse bridge. After that the route meanders up through broadleafed woods to Birks farmhouse, a remote and evocative spot with a fine view of the valley.

 **Getting there** *Birks Bridge car park and picnic area is on the Dunnerdale valley road, a couple of miles (3.2 km) from the junction at Cockley Beck where it leaves the Hardknott–Wrynose passes (about 12 miles (19 km) east of the A595).*

Length of walk 2 miles (3.2 km).
Time 1½ hours.
Terrain Riverside path and forest tracks. Could be managed by an all-terrain pushchair if you walk down the road to Birks Bridge instead of following the riverbank.
Start/Parking Birks Bridge free car park and picnic area (GR: SD234995).
Map OS Explorer OL6 The English Lakes (South-western area).
Refreshments The nearest pub is the Newfield Inn, 3 miles (4.8 km) down the valley in Seathwaite. Fortunately it's a gem, serving traditional meals and a good range of local beers.

◆ Fun Things to See and Do ◆

There are two main bridges on this walk, and a level footpath beside the river. That means it's ideal for Pooh ships. Now anyone can drop a twig one side of a bridge and race it to the opposite side – in **Pooh ships** you have to find something a bit more substantial that will run for the 330 yards (300 m) between the Forestry Commission bridge by the car park, and the ancient packhorse bridge downstream. And whose ship will make it all the way through the rapids? Fortunately there is no shortage of sticks in this forest. Can anyone find one that looks like an animal?

The Duddon Valley inspired the poet Wordsworth to write endless lines about how much he really liked the place. On your way up to Birks farm, or perhaps on the long forest road back down to the river, why not have a go at composing your own poem? And, remember, you can cheat a little to make it rhyme: 'On Duddon's brig, I found a twig; it won the race, which was really ace'.

Birks Bridge and Upper Dunnerdale

The Walk

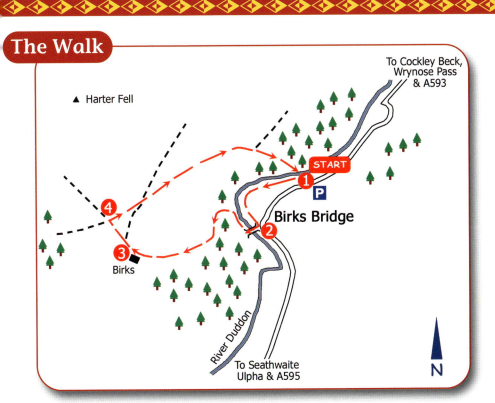

To Cockley Beck, Wrynose Pass & A593

▲ Harter Fell

START

P

Birks Bridge

Birks

River Duddon

To Seathwaite Ulpha & A595

N

1 From the Birks Bridge car park pick out a little riverside path by the bridge, on the opposite side of the track to the picnic tables. Follow this to its rather boggy conclusion above the rapids at Birks Bridge itself (NB: that's the stone bridge).

2 Cross the bridge and, through the gate, take the path on the far side that veers right to begin with then swings left, up the hill into the woods. Continue on the uphill line to reach a gate. Beyond this a walled lane heads up towards Birks farmhouse. Continue up the slope and go through the gateway into the former farmyard, bearing right in front of the gable end.

3 In front of the farm walk straight ahead through the access gate and over the cattle grid. Stay on the forest road to reach a junction.

4 Turn right, downhill, beneath the rocks of Buck Crag and stay on this good track as it re-enters the forest proper. The road leads pleasantly to the access bridge by the car park. Cross the bridge to return to the picnic area.

◆ Background Notes ◆

The **Hardknott Forest** was very controversial when the Forestry Commission planted it in the 1930s. It became a cause célèbre for the newly formed Friends of the Lake District, and though the Eskdale side of Harter Fell was eventually spared, the Dunnerdale forest stretched almost to the fell tops. But now the process is working in reverse and the forestry is being undone. Clearfelling has returned open space to the dale head and a new planting programme of traditional broadleaf trees is replacing the squared up masses of conifers. In the language of the day, the commercial trees were described by conservationists as 'goose-stepping ranks'.

The remote **Birks farmhouse** was bought by the Commission in the 1930s and lay derelict for many years until its lease was taken on by the Grove School from Market Drayton in the 1960s. The school uses it as a field study centre and bought the freehold of the property in 1985. Further up the valley, Wigan Borough runs another former farm, Hinning House, as an outdoor education centre.

William Wordsworth was taken fishing on the Duddon as a child, and though he caught very little, the memory inspired him to return to the valley as an adult. Eventually he created a series of 34 sonnets: 'Still glides the stream, and shall forever glide. The form remains, the function never dies' (After-thought. Sonnet 34, The River Duddon – A Series of Sonnets, 1820).

Following the tortuous road over the **Hardknott Pass** into Eskdale is worth the effort. Not only can you visit the magnificent **Roman fort** on the pass itself, but a few miles down the valley you'll come to the Dalegarth terminus of the **Ravenglass and Eskdale Railway**, the finest miniature railway in Britain (see Walk 9).

Giggle Alley and Eskdale Green

Japanese Bridges and a Miniature Railway

The route through Giggle Alley

There is something very special about Eskdale. Perhaps it's because of its delightful little railway, t'laal Ratty – always a hit with children – which unobtrusively chuffs up and down the valley from Dalegarth, near Boot to the sea at Ravenglass. Perhaps because it is one of the quietest of the Lakeland dales, its single track roads never experiencing the volumes of traffic you'd meet in Borrowdale or Langdale. Or maybe it's because it is unremittingly lovely at almost every turn, from the ring of high mountains to the coastal dunes and marshes. This walk takes a sumptuous taster slice from the middle of the dale, and in doing so reveals a bizarre hidden garden owned by the Forestry Commission, some fine views up to Scafell and of course allows you to see t'laal Ratty up close from the station at The Green.

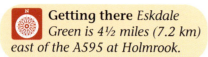

9

Getting there *Eskdale Green is 4½ miles (7.2 km) east of the A595 at Holmrook.*

Length of walk 2 miles (3.2 km).
Time 1½ hours.
Terrain Woodland tracks, fell paths and a quiet lane. Not really suitable for pushchairs.
Start/Parking Free car park in Eskdale Green by the entrance to the Forestry Commission's Giggle Alley and public toilet (GR: NY141002).
Map OS Explorer OL6 The English Lakes (South-western area).
Refreshments In Eskdale Green you have a choice of two lovely pubs. About 400 yds (366 m) to the west is the Bower House Inn, with a beer garden and play area and excellent local beers and

◆ Fun Things to See and Do ◆

The first thing to discover on this walk is the **Japanese Garden**. It's a very strange place with several tiny bridges and ponds, but you have to venture up into the woods and through a weird granite canyon to find it. It's a great place to explore. The whole garden is surrounded by tall bamboo thickets, so there are some brilliant places to hide. Look out for the frogs and toads in the ponds. The toads are usually the gnarly knobbly ones, whereas the frogs tend to be smoother skinned.

Beyond this the Castle Rocks are the first of **several granite outcrops to clamber over**. A bit later in the walk, the crags of Hollin How are a little more precipitous but older children will enjoy the challenges.

You can't visit Eskdale without a ride on **t'laal Ratty**. The miniature trains chug up and down the valley, often hauled by proper working tiny steam engines. You'll frequently hear the trains whistle before you see them. The up trains from The Green head for Dalegarth, the down trains leave the valley of the Esk and take the Miterdale side of Muncaster Fell to the terminus by the big railway at Ravenglass. There are displays, shops and cafés at both ends.

Giggle Alley and Eskdale Green

The Walk

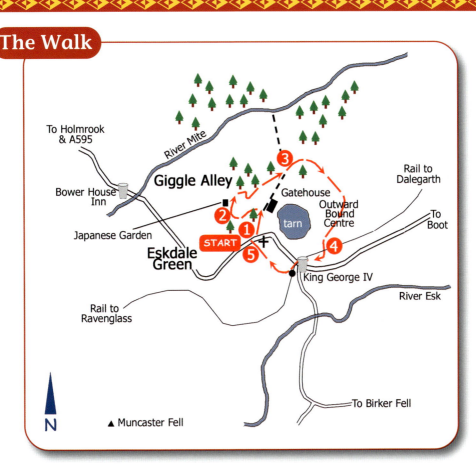

home-cooked food. It's matched in all ways, except the play area, by the King George IV, a similar distance in the opposite direction, beyond the station.

1 From the parking area by the public toilets walk up the rough lane, soon turning left into Giggle Alley's woodlands up a flight of steps. At the top of the steps turn left on a forest path, following it around to the right and up a bank to reach a granite staircase leading through a wall of rock.

2 Walk through the Japanese Garden, the paths all lead to the far side. Continue on a granite track, now descending amidst bamboo and rhododendrons. Soon a flight of steps lifts you back into the centre of the knoll and woodland opens out in Owl Glade. Continue on the obvious path through a gate and up to the craggy outcrop known as Castle Rocks. The path steers away to their left and continues, descending another stone staircase and traversing open woodland. At the far end go through a gate to a track junction.

3 Walk straight across here, going up the rough track by the side of the Gatehouse grounds. Beyond a gate at the top of the bank, turn right and follow the path, which tracks the edge of the Outward Bound centre. Passing over a little rise, the path descends away from Gatehouse now to a gate in the wall ahead. Follow the path around the summit of Hollin How until you meet a junction by a fence corner. Turn right here and continue downhill with a fence on your left. You pass several little practice crags before swinging left with the fence down to a gateway beside the delightful old farmhouse of Hollin How. Continue down a narrow path to join the access road.

4 Turn right and, crossing the railway bridge, walk out to the

So, where's the train?

road. Turn right, with care, for a few paces, then cross over to the entrance to the station and a bridleway. Continue past the station on the bridleway for a few hundred more paces, then bear right up the lane to the level crossing. Cross the railway with care and follow this track as it meanders between pleasant cottages and villas to emerge in the centre of the village.

5 Turn right to return to the parking area.

◆ Background Notes ◆

Giggle Alley's Japanese Garden was built for the Rea family of Gatehouse in 1914. The garden was designed by Lakeland garden guru Thomas Mawson, and by 1923 it was described as having been 'called into being as by a magician's wand'. Sadly James Rea, the passionate enthusiast who had commissioned the garden, died in 1918, and never saw it at its finest. The Gatehouse estate was finally sold off in 1949, with the Outward Bound Trust taking the house and garden for their first 'mountain school'. They were unable to maintain the Japanese Garden and it fell into decay. The Forestry Commission bought the site in 1961 along with surrounding woodlands and the garden disappeared into a dense undergrowth of rampant rhododendron and bamboo. It was rescued in 1999 by a group of local volunteers, who have painstakingly removed much of the excess plant cover, restored bridges and unblocked waterways. Now there is a proper plan for the garden's survival and growth in a truly special corner of the Lake District.

The **Ravenglass and Eskdale Railway** was originally opened in 1875 on a 3 ft gauge track to transport mine and quarry products to the main line at Ravenglass. It carried passengers from quite early on, advertising itself as a journey to the 'foot of Scawfell in the English Alps'. Scawfell is an alternative, and archaic, spelling of Scafell, which explains why the correct pronunciation of Scafell is 'Scawfell' After a number of financial problems it was converted to a 15 inch gauge in 1916 and the track has been on this smaller width ever since. Trains run all year round though the winter service is limited. The railway has also been known as t'laal Ratty (the little Ratty) since the narrow gauge trains replaced the 3 ft gauge in 1916. The original railway was known as Owd Ratty (old Ratty).

On the Edge of Wastwater

England's Deepest Lake

The boathouse seen at point 2 of the walk

This is an easy walk and gives you a chance to gaze at what was once voted Britain's best view, in a TV talent contest for views, from a convenient bench above an idyllic beach alongside England's deepest lake. The children also get to play in the woods, see some rare breeds on a working farm and scramble about amidst bracken and crag. Wastwater is as dramatic a lake as you'll find in Cumbria, filling the base of remote Wasdale for several miles. You can extend the walk slightly from the ancient Lund Bridge (point 3) to get a closer look at the magnificent screes that soar up from the far lakeshore. Going all the way round, though, is a job for experienced walkers only, with plenty of time on their side. We leave the lakeshore, following the River Irt for a short distance before heading off across farmland to Woodhow and Ashness How, every turn revealing another aspect of the breathtaking scenery.

On the Edge of Wastwater

Getting there *Wastwater is approached by minor roads from the A595 at Gosforth. Turn left after Nether Wasdale and the parking area is along the shoreside, a mile or so beyond the Youth Hostel.*

Length of walk 2 miles (3.2 km).
Time 1½ hours.
Terrain Tracks and field paths. Not really suitable for pushchairs. Some road walking at the beginning and end of the walk. Some parts of the walk can be very wet, especially after rain, so wellies might be a good idea.

Start/Parking There's a little roadside parking near the start of the walk (GR: NY150052). If it's full, you'll have to park further up the lake and walk down the road to the start.

Map OS Explorer OL6 The English Lakes (South-western area).

Refreshments There's nowhere on the walk, but the iconic Wasdale Head Inn is only a few miles up the valley, whilst Nether Wasdale village boasts two fine pubs in the Strands Hotel and the Screes Inn.

The Walk

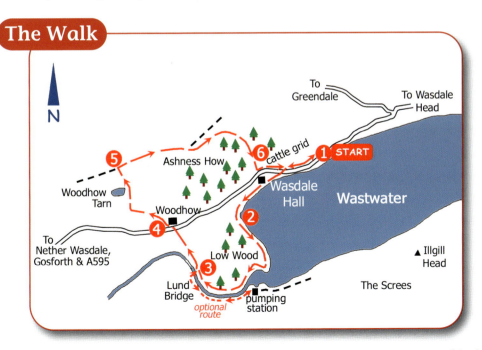

Kiddiwalks in Cumbria & the Lake District

1 From the roadside parking area, with your back to the lake, turn left and walk down the lake towards foot of the lake. Take care here as the traffic can be sporadic. Soon the road bears right, away from the lake, at a final parking pull-in. Leave the road here, finding a narrow descending path on your left towards a ladder stile in the wall ahead. Cross the stile, descending the steep steps beyond into a virtual tunnel of rhododendrons. Soon the path opens out, however, and you find yourself on a muddy path beside the lake. Follow this through a gate into a little wooded headland. Beyond this another gate leads into the parkland of Wasdale Hall, now a Youth Hostel.

2 Round a little bay beyond the

◆ Fun Things to See and Do ◆

In the grounds of Wasdale Hall you can go and **poke the old tree stumps**! There used to be some huge trees standing here but the National Trust has felled them because they were beginning to go rotten. Now they are home to several different types of burrowing insect and the largest stump is a superb nesting site for birds.

Beyond Wasdale Hall, **Low Wood** is open access land. The whole wood was once choked with dense rhododendrons but most of these have now been cleared, leaving a perfect open woodland with plenty of offcuts lying around for **den building**. If the level of the lake allows, there is a **lovely beach** here, facing up the valley to the iconic mountain profile reproduced in the National Park logo.

Woodhow Farm specialises in **rare breeds**. As you cross the knoll beside the farm you get a good look into the farmyard, where all manner of livestock are kept. In the surrounding fields you'll see pigs with different markings – some have spots, some have red hair. You should see goats and peculiar looking sheep too. How many different ones can you identify?

hall you'll find the path enters Low Wood and becomes a gentle avenue above a gravelly beach, with breathtaking views up the lake to the mountains at Wasdale Head. Stay with this path as it follows the shore, rounding a little headland to reveal a boathouse and a shallow bay opposite a barn-like structure on the far bank. The waterway to your left soon narrows to form the River Irt and your woodland path continues as a riverbank route, following the rightward sweep of the waters. Soon you come to a gate and a bridge.

One of the residents of Woodhow Farm

3 Go through the gate but don't cross the bridge unless you want to investigate the eastern shore of the lake. Instead stay by the waterside into a field and follow the path to another gate. Now climb up the grassy bank ahead to a metal kissing gate leading on to the road. Turn left and in a few paces cross over with care to the entrance to Woodhow Farm.

4 A footpath sign directs you through a pair of gates and over a little wooded bluff above the farmyard. On the far side join a farm track leading left towards fields. Soon bear right with a wall to reach a gate and then walk

along the field path towards Woodhow Tarn, which sadly isn't accessible. A further gate leads into an area of rougher pasture. The path reaches a T-junction by a large fallen tree.

5 Turn right here, along the base of a little crag and go through a gate into the access land of Ashness How. Follow the sometimes boggy track as it steers a course above the marsh. Ignore the first right turn, but beyond a funnel of gorse you'll see a marker post. Turn right here on a lesser path heading towards woodland. At the top of a rise the path appears to peter out, but persistence will reveal its indentation heading up a boggy slope in the direction of woodland. Rounding a little knoll, you'll see it leads to a ladder stile and a gate. Beyond this a walled track leads down to the road, passing Wasdale Hall's old walled garden on the left.

6 Turn left and walk along the road with care for 200 yds (183 m) to a cattle grid. Beyond this you will find the lakeside parking places.

◆ Background Notes ◆

Wastwater is England's deepest lake, the depths reaching nearly 260 ft (79 m). You oughtn't therefore to engage in too much paddling here, as it drops away very steeply only a few yards from the shore. The level of the lake was raised slightly to allow water extraction for the nuclear plant at Sellafield. The innocent looking barn you see on the opposite shore, emitting a low level hum, is actually the extraction pump house. The screes on the south-east shore rise up to nearly 2,000 ft (609 m) at Illgill Head, making this one of the most dramatic shorelines in Britain. The distinctive skyline at the top of the valley is made by the profiles of Yewbarrow (on the left), Great Gable (in the centre) and Lingmell (on the right). You can't actually see England's highest point from here, as Scafell Pike is hidden behind the shoulder of Illgill Head.

The **little island** just off the shore at the start is a favourite roost for black-headed gulls and other noisy seabirds.

Wasdale Hall was built in a mock-Tudor style in 1839 for Rawson Stansfield, a well-to-do banker from Halifax, West Yorkshire. It passed to the National Trust in 1959 and is now a Youth Hostel. You pass the house's old walled garden at the end of the walk. For an insight into what this might have once looked like, you can visit Monk Coniston, near Coniston, where the National Trust has been restoring the walled garden to its former glory.

Grasmere and Loughrigg Terrace

In the Footsteps of Poets

A dramatic view of Grasmere

This lovely walk incorporates a riverbank, woodland, meadows, a lake and even a beach, so there are plenty of fascinating things for the children to see and do as you go. Grasmere would be famous even if several poets hadn't landed here in the early 19th century, ensuring that it would never be short of visitors ever again. But despite the obvious popularity (you probably won't be alone on this walk) it is always pleasing. Not just because the views are breathtakingly lovely, or because you can find real places written about by Wordsworth and co, but because it is also unfailingly interesting. From the broad path across the meadows to begin with, into the atmospheric, root infested woods and on to a miniature peninsula, with its rocky-fingered outcrops into the dark waters of Grasmere Lake, to the magnificent balcony of Loughrigg Terrace and back into the spooky woodland, there isn't much to complain about at any stage. Even the up bits aren't too up, and the beach really is a gem.

Kiddiwalks in Cumbria & the Lake District

11

Getting there *White Moss car park is on both sides of the A591 between Rydal and Grasmere.*

(GR: NY348065). Toilets available.

Map OS Explorer OL7 The English Lakes (South-eastern area).

Length of walk 2½ miles (4 km).
Time 1½ hours.
Terrain Good paths through woods, meadows, open fell and lakeside. Not suitable for pushchairs.
Start/Parking White Moss lower car park, pay-and-display

Refreshments There's usually an ice-cream van perched on the corner of the road by the car park. For something more substantial, the Badger Bar at Rydal and the Old School Room tea shop at Rydal Hall are just down the road.

◆ Fun Things to See and Do ◆

There's something really spooky about the woods on this walk. They're all gnarly roots and lichen-covered branches. It's perfect for the version of **hide and seek** where you have to run ahead and jump out on the unsuspecting.

When you reach Grasmere lake you have a choice and you might want to do both. Straight ahead there's a little **rocky peninsula** sticking out into the lake, which deserves a careful exploration, but over the bridge there's a **beach** just right for skimming stones in the water, paddling or even making dams in one of the tiny becks.

Loughrigg Terrace is like a wide mountain road, only grassier, gently dipping away down the hill. If you're feeling sporty you can run down it, but mind the picnickers drinking their coffee!

Even the car park has things to explore. See if you can **find the tunnel**. Where does it go? You would need a strong torch and a good safety helmet to find out, so it's probably safer not to try.

The Walk

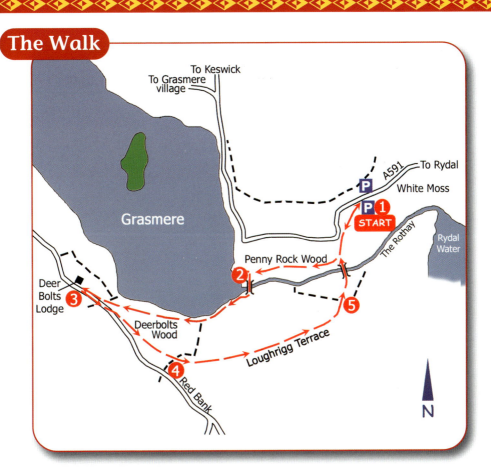

To Keswick
To Grasmere village

A591 — To Rydal

White Moss

P

P ① START

Grasmere

The Rothay

Rydal Water

Penny Rock Wood ②

Deer Bolts Lodge ③

Deerbolts Wood

Loughrigg Terrace ⑤

④ Red Bank

N

① From the lower White Moss car park and with your back to the road, walk to the right, through the trees and past the public toilets. Approaching a wooden bridge on the left, keep to the right, staying on the bank you are on and going through a gate into White Moss Woods and Meadow. On the far side of the meadow, go through the gate and continue on the obvious path through a clearing. Beyond this go through another gate into Penny Rock Wood. Staying on the path closest to the river, walk over a rise, then descend to another bridge at the outlet from Grasmere. There's a lovely view of the lake from a rocky promontory just beyond here, but return to the bridge and cross it.

2 Turn right, along a shoreline path. At the far end of the beach, go through either gate and take the rising path up into the woods. Where the path forks, take the left-hand option going up the hill. At the top of the path emerge at a little cabin in the woods known as Deer Bolts Lodge.

3 The road ahead of you is Red Bank, a back road route connecting Grasmere with Langdale. Don't go onto the road though, turn sharp left on a bridleway signposted to Loughrigg Terrace and Rydal. Pass through a wooden barrier and keep ahead to a pair of double gates. Beyond this you'll find a metal gate with a National Trust sign. The view now opens out as you begin the magnificent Loughrigg Terrace path.

4 Ignore the stepped route up to the right and stay on this gently descending path, passing several benches making good use of the unfolding panorama. Eventually, at a path junction, keep left, aiming for the trees ahead by a mini saddle. Bear right here,

Near the start of the walk

taking the downward path closest to the wall to discover two large slates and a gate on the left.

5 Squeeze between these into White Moss Woods and follow the descending path. Winding down through the woods and over little rises, this is perfect hide and seek territory. The path levels out at the riverside by the first bridge passed earlier. Cross over this time, turning right on the far side to return to the car park and toilets.

Grasmere and Loughrigg Terrace

William Wordsworth (born 1770) came to Grasmere in December 1799, moving into what became known as Dove Cottage with his sister Dorothy. She stayed with him after his marriage to Mary Hutchinson in 1802 and it was from this little house, now a museum, that he wrote his most famous verses. *Daffodils* was written as he walked back to Grasmere along the side of Ullswater having visited friends in Pooley Bridge. **Samuel Taylor Coleridge** tipped up in the area around the same time and **Thomas de Quincy** (born 1785) liked it so much he moved into Dove Cottage when the Wordsworths moved out in 1809. It's difficult to imagine this sleepy Lakeland community being at the cutting edge of literature, but for a while it was. Wordsworth eventually settled at Rydal Mount, dying there in 1850. De Quincy married Peggy Simpson from Nab Cottage (just by the road overlooking Rydal Water) and lived there until his opium addiction got the better of him. In 1832 he moved with his family to Edinburgh, where he died in 1859. The poets knew these woods and these fell and lake views. What they would make of their current popularity is anyone's guess.

You'll see several remnants of **quarry working** on this walk. Apart from poetry, slate was the Brathay valley's most lucrative export for many years and just beyond the end of the terrace path there's a massive cave. If you have time it's definitely worth a detour. The car park is partly built on old workings too, so keep an eye out for the occasional tunnel and open edge. Slates from here went all across northern England, until cheaper versions became available from North Wales.

Grasmere Lake, which gave its name to the village, is about 71 ft (around 21 m) deep in the middle – not particularly deep by Lake District standards. Along with half of Rydal Water it is actually owned by the Lowther Estate, but leased to the National Trust. Lowther connections stretch back a long way here, for it was the Earl of Lonsdale (the head of the estate) who employed Wordsworth's father, and secured William's position as 'Distributor of Stamps' in Westmorland, thus ensuring the poet had an income.

12

Stonethwaite and Langstrath

Splashing through the Streams

Langstrath valley

Plenty of satisfying sploshing is on offer on this route! The little hamlet of Stonethwaite sits at the end of the road heading up into the wild valley known as Langstrath. Beyond here you must leave the car behind, but the effort is richly rewarded. Stonethwaite Beck divides into two at the rocky knoll of Smithymire Island above a tumbling waterfall called Galleny Force. It's a lovely place to linger on a summer's afternoon. To get there we walk along the ancient bridleway that once took packhorses up Greenup Gill and over the top to Grasmere, or up the Langstrath (long valley) itself to the Stake Pass into Langdale (another long valley!). Packhorses must have been used to the wet, because this route splashes through several shallow becks on the way as well as a short stretch of bog, all of which make this a really good walk for wearing wellies.

Stonethwaite and Langstrath

 Getting there
Stonethwaite is off the main Borrowdale valley road, about 6½ miles (10.4 km) south of Keswick.

Length of walk 2½ miles (4 km).
Time 1½ hours.
Terrain Valley tracks, often stony and frequently wet, occasionally boggy, but a lot of fun if you're suitably shod. Not really suitable for pushchairs.
Start/Parking The parking area by the phone box in Stonethwaite (GR: NY262137). If it's full, park further back towards the primary school (but not in the pub car park).
Map OS Explorer OL4 The English Lakes (North-western area).
Refreshments The Langstrath Country Inn is an excellent spot for a meal or just a drink. There's a beer garden across the road, local beer and a wide-ranging menu including an imaginative children's version.

◆ Fun Things to See and Do ◆

Splashing your way through the **countless little streams** that cross the outward route is great fun. In some places you can build little dams and make tiny ponds. If the water levels in the main becks are low you can paddle around Smithymire, but be careful after rain – it can turn into a raging torrent. On the return leg (after the third bridge) there's a wood where you can **make a den**.

This is a good walk to do in the rain, but if it all gets too much then head down the valley back to **Keswick** where you'll find the genuinely interesting **Pencil Museum**, which tells the story of the valley's graphite industry and even has special hollow pencils used by secret agents during the war. Another wet weather attraction is the Puzzling Place, where all manner of illusions will baffle and confuse you. Keswick has some good parks, including a playground for older children (besides the usual 3–10 version) and a leisure pool with a wave machine and flume.

12

The Walk

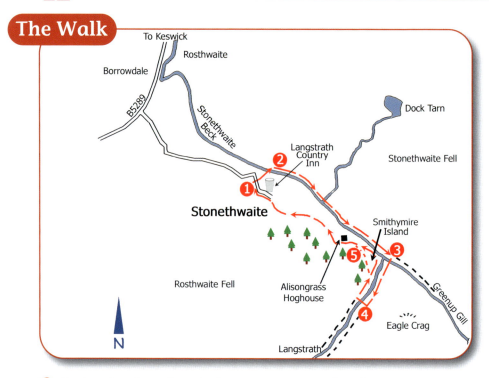

1 Facing the phone box in the centre of the village by the parking area, pick out the track to the left, which runs beside a cottage then out between stone walls to a bridge. Cross this and on the far side continue on the walled track to a gate. Beyond this, turn right at the signposted junction. You're now on the Cumbria Way, heading in the direction of Grasmere and Greenup Edge.

2 Go through another gate and walk up the valley with the wall on your right. The distinctive crag ahead is Eagle Crag. Beyond the next gate the way ahead may seem confusing at first but it is really very straightforward. All the tracks lead to the same place. At the far end of the field, cross the wooden bridge and continue across the next field to a gate. Through this one, continue ahead, now back on an enclosed track towards some yew trees. Splash across a little beck and beyond the final yew tree continue slightly uphill with the wall and river on your right. Go

Stonethwaite and Langstrath

through another gate and you'll see the riverside has opened out to give you a glimpse of the waterfalls known as Galeny Force.

3 Beyond some sheep pens, the left-hand path continues up Greenup, but we take the right-hand option through a gate and descending to a bridge over the river. Cross the bridge and walk up the bank on the far side. Tracks seem to head off in all directions, but you want to maintain your direction from the bridge. The way ahead now is prone to being very boggy. There are drier portions, and picking out a raised and solid route can be quite fun. Leaving the riverbank briefly, a wall comes between you and the beck. More boggy patches soon lead to

another bridge on the right.

4 Cross this and turn right down the track into the woods. Go through a gate and the way descends on a rocky path to a junction. You could bear left, but alternatively you get another chance to explore the riverside from here, by keeping straight ahead and following an obvious route with the water on your right. This meets up with the 'short-cut' path on your left, which would have conveyed you more swiftly to the same spot.

5 Now follow the walled track past Alisongrass Hoghouse and the campsite all the way back into Stonethwaite. Keep ahead on the road past the Langstrath Country Inn to return to the parking area.

◆ Background Notes ◆

In medieval times **Stonethwaite** was an outpost of Fountains Abbey. Today the Langstrath's bridleway is used by the **Cumbria Way**, a long-distance trail that runs for nearly 70 miles (112 km) from Ulverston to Carlisle.

In the second part of the walk you pass the intriguingly-named **Alisongrass Hoghouse** where medieval farmers kept their year-old sheep (hogs) over the winter, feeding them on hay, holly and bracken from the surrounding slopes and meadows.

13

Buttermere Village and Crummock Water

Secret Beaches and Hidden Woods

Setting off on an adventure!

B uttermere is best known for the lake that shares its name. And it's a lovely walk all the way round its shore. But sometimes you want something slightly different, a shorter walk with plenty of chance to play on the beach, perhaps. This little circuit takes you away from Buttermere to one of the valley's other beautiful lakes. Crummock Water is less well known, but the shoreline at the head of the lake is as lovely a spot as you will find in the Lake District. It's great for a paddle in summer, or a leisurely picnic, and you probably won't be fending off the crowds. There's a quite accessible shoreline backed in places by knobbly rises of woodland, and despite the access, it all feels very secret and hidden.

◆ 64

Buttermere Village and Crummock Water

 Getting there *You can approach Buttermere from three sides. The main road, the B5289, comes up from Cockermouth or the Whinlatter Pass, through Lorton and along the shores of Buttermere. From the top of the valley it comes from Borrowdale over the Honister Pass, or you can drop down into the middle of the village by the tiny road that snakes over the Newlands Pass from Braithwaite or Portinscale.*

Length of walk 2½ miles (4 km).

Time 1 hour (excluding stops).
Terrain Woodland trail, field paths and a short stretch of road at the end. Could be managed by an all-terrain pushchair with some help.
Start/Parking The National Trust car park, Buttermere village (GR: NY172172).
Map OS Explorer OL4 The English Lakes (North-western area).
Refreshments A choice of cafés and pubs in Buttermere village – Syke Farm serves delicious home-made ice-cream as well as teas and coffees.

◆ Fun Things to See and Do ◆

The **woods of Long How and Nether How are perfect for hiding in**. Nether How is especially good because the walk goes all the way round it, so whichever direction you go in, you'll always end up back on the track. At the far end of Nether How you'll find a beach. It's not the sandy sort, but the shaly pebbles are still quite good for digging in. You'll also find an abundance of **skimming stones**, but you might want to start collecting these before you get to the lake.

When you've finished the walk, it's worth making the trip up to the top of the Honister Pass, where you can visit the **working slate quarry**. It's a surprisingly good day out to join one of the mine tours, or even test your wits against the famous Via Ferrata – a metal walkway across the face of the towering crags (older children – over 10 – and adults only).

Kiddiwalks in Cumbria & the Lake District

The Walk

1 From the back of the car park, go through the kissing gate into the National Trust's woodlands of Long How. A good track leads up to a junction. Turn left and continue, downward now, eventually to some rocky steps leading to the riverbank. Turn right and follow the riverside path to a bridge.

2 Cross this and, in the field beyond, turn right, staying by the side of the beck. The path swings up into the woodlands of Nether How, a little rocky hillock, before dropping you down gently on to one of Crummock Water's most delightful beaches. It's mostly pebbles and rocks, but the setting is truly magnificent.

3 When you have finished playing here – and there is plenty to explore so you could take some time – follow the path around the base of Nether How. You will find a little rocky step to negotiate at the far end. The path swings back inland around the hill, eventually returning you to the riverside near the bridge you crossed earlier. Turn right, retracing your steps briefly, but don't cross the bridge. This time stay on the riverside path on the field side, to reach a gate.

4 Beyond this you'll see the campsite on the opposite bank.

Soon you arrive in Buttermere's National Park car park, where there are toilets. Walk out to the junction beyond the Fish Inn and turn left up the road. At the next junction, by the Bridge Hotel, turn left, taking care as you are now on the main valley road, for about 200 yds (183m) to return to the car park.

◆ Background Notes ◆

Crummock Water is the Lake District's 12th largest lake by area, being 2½ miles (4 km) long and ¾ mile (1.2 km) across. The deepest section is 140 ft (43 m). Take care if you're paddling as beyond the shallows of the bay at the head of the lake it drops away quite steeply. Below Rannerdale Knotts, where the road squeezes around a blasted shelf in the rock, the lake bottom drops some 70 ft in just a few yards. Both Crummock Water and Buttermere lakes are glacial in origin, the last ice having retreated up to the head of the valley as recently as 10,000 years ago. The main period of glaciation, though, was around 18,000 years ago, when the valley would have been filled by a vast glacier, deepening and steepening the valley sides and leaving rounded features like **Nether How** in its wake. Here, harder rocks were scraped and shaped by the passing ice. It's likely that the two lakes were once joined, but in the last 3,000 years or so the middle land has silted up, been drained and farmed.

In the golden age of tourism that preceded the First World War, the Buttermere hotels kept a veritable fleet of rowing boats to take visitors across Crummock Water to the mouth of the Scale Beck. Here they would disembark and tramp up the fellside to view **Scale Force**, the longest single-drop waterfall in England.

14

Whinlatter Forest

Nature Trails and Other Tails

Will we see one of those?

Have you ever wondered what the phrase 'we can't tell the wood from the trees' means? It's one of those odd things that people say, when they're a bit lost. Well this is a walk with loads of trees, and quite a lot of wood too, but hopefully we won't get lost. Whinlatter is a working forest, where the Forestry Commission cuts down hundreds of pine trees and stacks them up by the side of the tracks, waiting for huge lorries to come and take them away. But there isn't so much money in wood any more. There are cheaper, bigger forests in Finland and Canada that can supply all the wood we need for building houses and making paper. This is great news for us, because now we can play in the forest more safely. While you're here, you'll see mountain bikers, rope course walkers, birdwatchers and tea shop visitors, as well as plenty of walkers enjoying the quieter parts of the woodland.

Whinlatter Forest

Getting there *Whinlatter Forest visitor centre is on the B5292, about 5 miles west of Keswick, at the top of the Whinlatter Pass.*

Length of walk 2½ miles (4 km).
Time Allow 2 hours.
Terrain Forest tracks and paths with a few steep descents. Not suitable for pushchairs.
Start/Parking The pay-and-display car park at the Whinlatter Forest visitor centre (GR: NY207244). Toilets at the Siskins café.
Map OS Explorer OL4 The English Lakes (North-western area) or the Whinlatter Forest map available from the visitor centre.
Refreshments The Siskins café at the visitor centre has a lovely balcony overlooking a series of birdfeeders, as well as the valley below, and is open daily.

◆ Fun Things to See and Do ◆

The biggest attraction is the **play area** – a fine, free to enter adventure playground with an aerial runway, model forestry vehicles to scramble over and plenty of other things to climb up and hang on to. Older children (over tens) and grown-ups might be tempted by the Go Ape! course, a much bigger (and more expensive) version in the trees above.

In the visitor centre you can watch live pictures of the **ospreys** nesting in the valley below in season.

On the walk itself, see if you can find the **lost dam**. When do you think it burst? What was it built in the forest for?

As well as spotting **squirrels**, **birds** and the occasional **deer**, don't be afraid to poke around in rotten tree stumps to see what lives in there. Often you'll find it's the home of a **stag beetle** – the antler-like horns are actually the mandibles (jaws) of the males.

The Walk

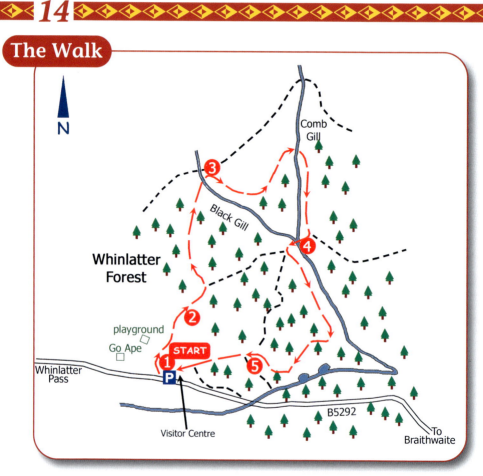

N

Comb Gill

Black Gill

Whinlatter Forest

playground

Go Ape

Whinlatter Pass

START

P

Visitor Centre

B5292

To Braithwaite

1 From the front of the visitor centre walk round the back of the café and pick out the trail sign by the rangers' office with the red, blue and green splodged marker. Follow the trail into the woods. Look for the peculiar markers, and follow the red green and blue flashes, taking a left turn soon, where it isn't obvious which way to go. A viewpoint soon opens out with a panel all about squirrels. The green trail disappears off into the woods but on the far side of the clearing stay with the red and green as they descend again.

2 Joining a forestry road, turn left on a forest track with the green and red marker. As you approach a bend in the track, the blue trail dives down to the right.

Continue with the red trail as it descends more gently. Keep with the red markers to a junction and another marker post, number 1. A contouring forest road now leads you over Black Gill.

3 Just beyond the gill a red post leads you back down into the woods. Descend now by the side of Black Gill, towards Comb Gill. A steeper section is perfectly manageable and the path levels out approaching a deer fence. Go through the big gate and beyond this the path loops round in a clear felled area, before crossing the gill and descending on the far side to another gate. As the track sweeps up the far side of the gill, pick up the red trail turning steeply right down the side of the beck before crossing over near the bottom by another gate. The trail continues to descend, now to a forest road with multiple waymarks.

4 Now you want to pick up the blue marker, to the right, across the road. Follow the trail continuing down by the side of the beck. Stay with the blue markers over a track and down into darker woodland. Through a stone enclosure, cross a bridge and at the next junction, turn right with the blue post. A viewpoint over a little stone gorge is followed by an upward path and a sharp right turn above an old dam. Keep on through younger trees, meandering past a pair of tiny ponds on the left. As you walk back up the hill, you meet a larger track, heading up the valley. On the far side of the bend pick up another blue post, and take a track, which becomes steeper, heading for the woods.

5 At the woodland edge turn left, now rejoining the red and green trails. Follow all three colours back to the visitor centre.

◆ Background Notes ◆

The Forestry Commission's **Whinlatter Forest** is England's only 'mountain' forest, with the planted tree line extending to over 1,600 ft (488 m) in places. Most of the trees are coniferous Norway and Sitka spruce, and Japanese larch. Much of the wood is sent to a paper mill in Workington, whilst branch material is sent to a wood-fired power station. The **ruined dam and small ponds** you pass midway through the walk once powered a lead mine at Thornthwaite.

Keswick and Brundholme Wood

Playing at Trains

Looking towards Blencathra

On 4th March 1972, the last passenger train rumbled out of Keswick station heading for Penrith and a line that had run for 100 years finally closed. This walk is great for recreating those old railway days – it even begins by the old platform in Keswick before taking you under bridges and over bridges on a wonderfully level walkway. But the route isn't all level. On the way out you soon scoot off into Brundholme Wood and one of those up-and-down paths that can be really good fun. Below you the rushing River Greta tumbles through a wooded valley and you quickly forget trains and even the A66, whose dramatic viaduct you pass under twice. On the return journey you pick up the railway line again, taking in several more bridges and other bits of railway ephemera before the railway path dives off left on a lovely boardwalk, high above the Greta Gorge below.

Keswick and Brundholme Wood

Length of walk 4 miles (6.4 km).
Time 2 hours.
Terrain Woodland paths and the disused railway line. The line is level and a popular cycling route; it makes a worthwhile there-and-back outing with a pushchair. The rest of the walk is not really suitable for pushchairs. At point 4 the route descends 120 steps, but this section can be avoided, if preferred. Some paths are narrow with a steep drop on one side, so care should be taken with younger children.
Start/Parking The car park by Keswick Leisure Pool, Station Avenue (GR: NY271237). There are toilets on the old station platform.
Map OS Explorer OL4 The English Lakes (North-western area).
Refreshments There's usually an ice-cream van down on Station Road and the Leisure Pool has a café, otherwise it's a 5-minute pavement walk into the centre of Keswick.

The Walk

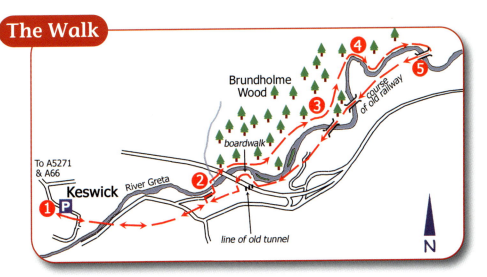

Brundholme Wood

course of old railway

boardwalk

To A5271 & A66

Keswick

River Greta

line of old tunnel

N

73

1 From the Keswick Pool car park, walk along the disused railway line, crossing the road and the River Greta by the first of several bridges. Pass under a bridge and in about 50 paces turn left, over the embankment and down a flight of steps to join a quiet lane. Turn right along the lane, then left as you approach the viaduct ahead.

2 Cross the Greta again and turn right, into the woods, through the kissing gate and past the 'Brundholme Woods' sign. Ignore the steps left and continue on the muddy path as it follows the bank of the river under the vast Greta viaduct carrying the A66 overhead. The path is narrow and drops away steeply on one side so do take extra care. After several ups and downs, the path descends to a more level area where there is a beach for skimming stones. Leaving this flatter area, ascend slightly, still with the river on your right. Eventually you rise to a footpath sign, offering a swift return to Keswick by turning right and crossing the river to rejoin the railway path. We take the left-hand option signposted towards Latrigg.

◆ Fun Things to See and Do ◆

Playing at trains is the best game, from the platform at Keswick to begin with, then under bridges and over bridges on the way back – looking out for the old platform at Low Briery, the wayside huts and the peculiar inverted 'bowstring' bridges.

There are **several good beaches** on the River Greta where stones can be skimmed, dams and waterways built, and dippers and kingfishers can be spotted.

Brundholme Wood is classic **red squirrel territory**, so keep your eyes peeled for these cute and surprisingly noisy little tree dwellers.

At the end of the walk, a few paces beyond the Leisure Pool, you'll find a really good **playground in Fitz Park**.

Keswick and Brundholme Wood

3 Follow the level path, contouring above the river and crossing a little bridge. The woods become more of oak and beech, then open out after a bend in the river. Maintain your direction, still up and down, but as you round a huge bend in the river, a flight of steps leads down to a viewpoint above some rapids (you can miss this out if you like by carrying straight on here, rejoining the route in a few hundred yards).

4 Over 120 steps deposit you on a level path by the river. Stay with the riverbank past several delightful picnic beaches. Continue round the bend, following the river, back up the slope to rejoin a crossing path.

Turn right and at the side of a field on the right, cross a stile and descend through the field to another stile leading to steps to the railway path.

5 Turn right and follow the railway path all the way back to the start. Beyond the caravan site there's a fine view of the shapely peaks of Blencathra to your rear. Here the line once disappeared into a tunnel. This has been filled in and the path instead rounds the hill on a magnificent boardwalk, to emerge in a meadow beneath the Greta viaduct. Walk under the bridge, past the Sustrans Millennium marker, rejoining the original course of the railway back into Keswick.

◆ Background Notes ◆

The **Keswick Railway Path** is a part of the popular C2C (Sea to Sea) route connecting Whitehaven to Sunderland. It's particularly popular at weekends, so do look out for cyclists. It follows the trackbed of the old Cockermouth, Keswick and Penrith Railway, which opened in 1865 and closed in 1972. Significant parts of the line were almost immediately re-used for the A66 trunk road, controversially built through the heart of northern Lakeland and opened in 1976. The Greta viaduct was completed in 1977. The station building was taken over by the adjacent hotel and now the platform provides a peculiar link with the past, as well as a handy location for a public toilet. **Brundholme Wood** belongs to the Mirehouse Estate and once supplied timber to the bobbin mills in the valley bottom.

16

Keldas and Lanty's Tarn

To the Secret Lake

The view from the summit of Keldas

Lanty's Tarn is a tiny secret lake, hidden amongst trees and crags above Glenridding, perfect for hide and seek. You won't see it until you're almost standing on its shore, but when you do, you won't want to leave – and it's a lovely spot to linger for a picnic. Getting there, and to the neighbouring summit of Keldas, with its spectacular view of Ullswater snaking away at your feet, is surprisingly straightforward. Below you, Glenridding has a proper resort feel, with a playground and boat hire, cafés and pubs, souvenir shops and a tourist information centre.

Keldas and Lanty's Tarn

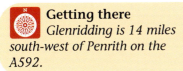

Getting there
Glenridding is 14 miles south-west of Penrith on the A592.

Length of walk 2 miles (3.2 km).
Time 2 hours.
Terrain There's nearly 500 ft (152 m) of ascent from Glenridding up to Keldas. The way up is relatively gentle but the way down again is quite steep, though mostly grass and bracken. The paths are good, especially on the more level sections. Not suitable for pushchairs.
Start/Parking Glenridding pay-and-display car park (GR: NY385169); toilets and visitor centre.
Map OS Explorer OL5 The English Lakes (North-eastern area).

The Walk

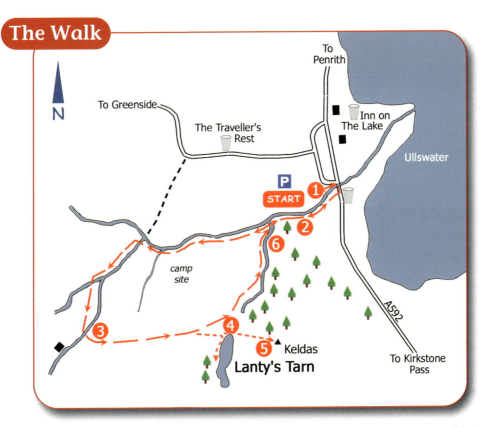

Refreshments There's a good choice of cafés and pubs in Glenridding.

1 From the car park, walk out, past the tourist information centre and toilets and turn right along the pavement and over the bridge. Turn right again, with the beck now on your right, and walk up the lane, passing the village hall.

2 In ¼ mile (400 m), take the right-hand fork, dropping down to a riverside path and continuing beside a campsite. Leave the riverside by turning left up a lane, climbing steeply in front of a cottage. As the track levels, look for a tiny signpost and a path descending left to cross a beck. On the far side rise to a gate and bear right with the contouring path.

3 Continue on this line across the slope, passing between a dramatic boulder and the slope. Rounding the bend you'll reach a gate. Go through this and rise more gently to a brow. From here descend to a gate by a wall in the woods.

4 To visit the summit of Keldas, don't go through this gate but carry straight on, rising steeply on an obvious path to a jumble of rocks on the little summit. There are great views from here, up the valley and down the lake to the distant Pennines.

5 Retrace your steps down the steep slope to the gate by the woods. Lanty's Tarn is on the other side of this wall, bounded

◆ Fun Things to See and Do ◆

Look for the **boulder pass** on the way up. The path traverses the hillside, at one point seeming to divide an enormous rock from the rest of the hill.

Lanty's Tarn is fairly sheltered and a good point for skimming stones.

From the summit of **Keldas**, you can look down on the village below and trace the whole of your route to the top.

by woods. *You can extend the walk by a couple of miles if you wish, by following the tarnside path, then descending into Grisedale by the kennels and returning on a footpath alongside the A592 into Patterdale then Glenridding, with more lovely views along the way.* Otherwise retrace your steps a little further and take the path descending right, going down steeply towards woodland and a gate. Continue descending until you emerge from the woods by some buildings.

6 Now follow the access lane down more gently to rejoin your original outward route. Turn right and walk back into Glenridding, turning left at the main road to reach the car park.

◆ Background Notes ◆

Glenridding grew as a mining settlement. Lead and other ores were mined in this area from the 16th century. The rows of miners' cottages can be seen on the opposite side of the valley from this walk.

The largest mine was **Greenside** – you can see the workings up to your left as you look across Glenridding's valley from the higher points of the walk. In the late 1950s this mine played a peculiar role in Cold War nuclear arms negotiations. Scientists from the Atomic Weapons Research Establishment exploded over a ton of TNT deep down in the old workings, taking seismic measurements as far away as Malham in the Yorkshire Dales. The readings were used to show that an explosion as large as a nuclear blast could be hidden from observers if it was detonated in a chamber of a certain size. The test, which used conventional explosives, was a success and had an impact on the negotiations in Geneva, but sadly two miners died in a different part of the mine, overcome by poisonous fumes. It was the last drama of the 300-year-old mine, which finally closed in 1962.

Lanty is a short form of Lancelot, and the valley's history records a number of characters who may have given their name to the tarn. The most likely is perhaps Lancelot Dobson, whose family owned much of Grisedale in the 18th century.

Hallin Fell

A Proper Mountain!

My first mountain path!

It would be a shame to walk in the Lake District without touching a proper summit at least once. Hallin Fell is a proper summit, with proper views and a quartet of pages in Wainwright's guide to the Far Eastern Fells to prove it. But there's a neat trick involved in getting to the top without too much aggravation. The steep, winding road that passes over Martindale Hause brings you within 600 ft (183 m) and half a mile (800 m) of the top. This short circular walk offers wide grassy slopes, brackeny hummocks and plenty of scope for pathside mini-adventures. There's a steep bit at the beginning, but it doesn't last long and the views from the summit may just about convert even the most reluctant young walker into an aspiring alpinist.

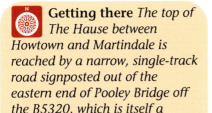 **Getting there** *The top of The Hause between Howtown and Martindale is reached by a narrow, single-track road signposted out of the eastern end of Pooley Bridge off the B5320, which is itself a turning off the A592.*

Length of walk 1½ miles (2.4 km).
Time 1½ hours.
Terrain Open fell, mostly grass bracken and bog. Not suitable for pushchairs.
Start/Parking The lay-by opposite St Peter's church, The Hause, Martindale (GR: NY435192).
Map OS Explorer OL5 The English Lakes (North-eastern area).
Refreshments In summer the Howtown Hotel has a small non-residents' bar and offers traditional meals. For the rest of the year, you will have to retreat to Pooley Bridge, where there is a range of pubs and cafés.

◆ Fun Things to See and Do ◆

 First you have to get up the hill. The big grassy bank might seem a bit off-putting (you can't see the top at first), but it's an ideal place for '**uphill golf**'. Spot a feature in the middle distance (say 50 yds/46 m) and guess how many steps it will take to get there. You get points for being the closest (or you lose points for every step you missed by). When you're past this bit there are lots of bracken-clad little **side summits to conquer on the way** and when you get to the end of the boggy valley, the view is like being in an aeroplane. Look for the **steamers on the lake below**. There are several different ones to spot, the newest being the *Western Belle*, which came into service in 2011. You can catch a steamer from the pier at Howtown at the bottom of the winding road up to the Hause. To the right it goes back to Pooley Bridge, and to the left it disappears round the corner to Glenridding.

At 1,273 ft (388 m) Hallin Fell is a '**Wainwright**' and you can tick it off – just 213 more to go.

The Walk

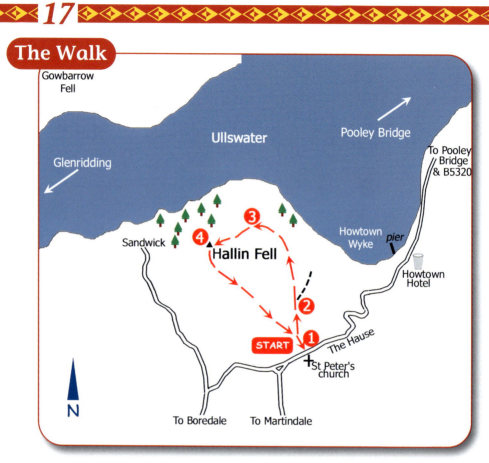

1 First you face the steep grassy slope opposite St Peter's church at the top of the Hause. Walk up the slope – it really isn't that far. From the top of the bank much of the rest of your route can be seen: you're going out to the right and coming back down the left. At a junction of paths take the right-hand option, passing a water supply structure then a big boulder before going over the brow. The way up through the bracken might seem a little relentless at first but you soon get into a stride. This is a good place to play 'uphill golf'.

2 Choose the upward path to the left at your next junction and a couple of cairns guide you. At the top of a rise, you'll see the path levels out. Now take the right-hand path, maintaining

Hallin Fell

your direction (though a grassy peak to the right is worth a quick detour). Keeping to the left of a boggy area you finally reach a path T-junction with a view facing the lake.

3 Turn left, tracking up the hill into a shallow gully, with the lake to your back. As the gully opens out, the surprisingly large summit pillar comes into view on the far side of a grassy hollow. Cross the hollow to make the last little pull to the top, with airy views up and down Ullswater on one side and up the valleys of Martindale and Boredale on the other.

4 The descent is short and sweet, and hard not to do at a jog. Beyond the summit (to the south-west) a path leads down into another grassy hollow. Stay with it and you'll find it channels you into a valley before swinging left and taking a direct route down the grass and bracken fellside. Maintain your direction, the trees surrounding St Peter's church acting as a guide. You're eventually joined by a wall on your right before reaching the junction passed on your outward route. Bear right down the grassy bank to the parking area.

◆ Background Notes ◆

There are very few hills over 1,000 ft (305 m) that can be reached relatively painlessly, but this is one. **Hallin Fell** appears in 'A Pictorial Guide to the Lakeland Fells, Book Two – The Far Eastern Fells' by Alfred Wainwright. Wainwright described it as 'the motorists' fell', commenting that the trippers from Carlisle and Penrith (he was writing in the 1950s, remember) demonstrated good taste in choosing such a fine hill as an easy destination. There are 214 'Wainwrights' in the Lake District and visiting all their summits has become a popular challenge.

The parish **church of St Peter**, which sits on the Hause, is not the highest in the county, but is surely one of the most remote. It was built in 1880 to replace the far simpler building (St Martin's) down in the valley bottom.

18

Appleby-in-Westmorland

Round the Bend

The River Eden

This lovely riverside walk takes you on both sides of the large bend in the River Eden at Appleby, with parkland on one side and a wood with red squirrels on the other. Appleby-in-Westmorland is perhaps best known for its New Fair – a dramatic meeting of traditional gypsy travellers to trade horses and stories every June. For the rest of the year it is a quiet little town. Its main street stretches up to the castle on the top of the hill, showing off its medieval origins and a fetching array of other period buildings in the process. This site on the river is also the town's biggest headache, for just as surely as the Romanies come to set up camp in June, so the winter floods threaten the surrounding streets with icy brown water. As well as the shallows on The Sands where horses are traditionally washed in the river, look out for the flood barriers that surround the central grid of streets to keep the water out.

Getting there *Appleby is off the A66, between Penrith and Scotch Corner. The centre of town is across the river from The Sands and Bongate, approached over the Eden Bridge. To find the car park, drive into the centre of the town and turn right alongside the church. The car park is at the end of this road.*

Length of walk 2 miles (3.2 km).
Time 1 hour.
Terrain Woods and riverside paths. Suitable for all-terrain pushchairs.
Start/Parking Chapel Street pay-and-display car park, Appleby-in-Westmorland (GR: NY682203). There are toilets here.
Map OS Explorer OL19 Howgill Fells & Upper Eden Valley, or

◆ Fun Things to See and Do ◆

There is a **children's play area** at the start (and end) of the walk, with a reasonable collection of swings and climbing frames for younger children – and with a plastic dolphin guarding the entrance.

When you get into the woods, if you're quiet, you may be lucky and spot a **red squirrel**. They are quite common here. By the river keep an eye open for a long-legged **heron**, standing guard over the fish stocks.

See how many **different types of flood barrier** you can spot. The most dramatic ones are by the swimming pool car park. Look carefully and you'll see that they rise up from the road.

If you have the energy, you can walk up to the **castle** and peer through the gates. Unfortunately the castle is closed to the public at the moment, but you should be able to catch a glimpse of its turrets as you walk round the town. It was built in 1092, when this part of Cumbria had only just transferred from Scotland to England.

If you enjoy trains, a trip on the **Settle-to-Carlisle railway** is a must. Appleby station is on a hill above the old part of town.

18

Appleby street map from the tourist information centre.
Refreshments The centre of Appleby has several pubs and cafés serving food at most times of the day. Close to the start of the walk, the Taste of Eden on Low Wiend is a good place for children.

1 From the parking area on Chapel Street, walk through the gateway between the lion and the unicorn and the flood barrier and walk down an avenue of beech trees. The children's play area is on the right. Can you see the dolphin litterbin? Tearing yourself away from here (you come back to this point later), walk down to the river and turn left along the riverside path.

The Walk

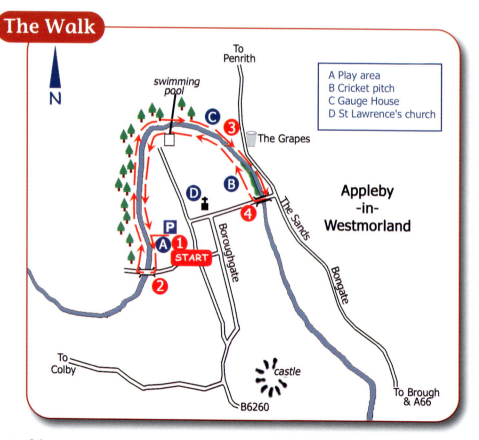

To Penrith

swimming pool

N

C

3

The Grapes

A Play area
B Cricket pitch
C Gauge House
D St Lawrence's church

D

B

4

P

A 1

START

2

Boroughgate

The Sands

Appleby
-in-
Westmorland

Bongate

To Colby

castle

B6260

To Brough
& A66

2 Reaching a bridge over the Eden, turn right, across the bridge, and immediately right again, signposted towards the Grammar School and The Sands. Go through a metal kissing gate and cross a short field to enter a wood. Now follow the obvious path ahead, alongside the river. When you get to a point opposite the swimming pool on the far bank, a series of shallow steps leads up into the woods. Another flight of steps takes you down again to the riverbank by a weir. Leaving the woodland, follow the path past the Gauge House and the old Pump House to reach The Sands by the Grapes pub.

3 Continue walking along The Sands by the pavement, until you get to the bridge. Turn right and cross the River Eden.

4 On the far bank, turn right again, through the flood barrier to join the riverside path, now on the opposite bank from before. Pass the graveyard and the cricket club, staying with the path as it follows the river bend all the way round and back to the children's play area. Turn left to return to the car park.

◆ Background Notes ◆

Appleby is a former county town and adopted 'in-Westmorland' in 1974 when Westmorland County Council was abolished. The Town Council still meets in the Moot Hall above the tourist information centre. The fine castle is at the top of Boroughgate but is not currently open to the public.

You'll see several places on this walk where the **flood defences** have become quite sophisticated – pop-up barriers, a monitoring station (Gauge House) and some very ornate gates now spring into action when the Environment Agency's flood warnings come.

The **New Fair week** is the first in June and, unless you enjoy crushing hordes, it's a good idea to avoid this time. The main event takes place on Fair Hill on the eastern side of town beyond the bypass. The Sands is the traditional washing place for horses and gets particularly busy, but there are usually horses almost everywhere.

Lacy's Caves and the River Eden

Sandstone Secrets

This is good fun!

The only there-and-back walk in this book, Lacy's Caves have long held a fascination for visitors old and young. They date from a time when Georgian gentlemen would pay for a local man to live as a hermit, somewhere on their estate, for the delight and entertainment of house guests. Here it was Colonel Lacy of Salkeld Hall in nearby Little Salkeld. The sandstone caves are certainly dramatic and make a great spooky destination, as long as you're careful. Children will enjoy finding the secret hiding place in the end chamber. The riverside here is lovely enough to stand a return journey the same way, with views opening out across the valley as you return to Daleraven, and a splendid fallen tree to climb at the beginning and end of the walk. There are usually buzzards circling above the woods and the overall effect is quite captivating.

Lacy's Caves and the River Eden

Getting there *Daleraven Bridge is a mile (1.6 km) or so south of Kirkoswald off the B6413. Turn right as you come into the village from the A6 and it's beyond Mains Farm.*

Length of walk 1½ miles (2.4 km).
Time 1½ hours.

Terrain Riverbanks and woodland with some steep drops. Midway the path was notoriously quagmire-like until enlightened interests oversaw the construction of a boardwalk across the worst bits – slippery in places, so watch out! Not suitable for pushchairs.
Start/Parking The lay-by next to Daleraven Bridge (GR: NY565395).

◆ Fun Things to See and Do ◆

The big draw for this walk is **the caves** at the end. They may seem dark and spooky at first, but if you shut your eyes for 30 seconds, once you are inside, then open them again, you'll be able to see more clearly.

Look for the **fallen tree** at the top of the bank at the start of the walk. It came down in the great storm of 2005 and now makes a brilliant natural climbing frame.

The **boardwalk** halfway to the caves takes the path above some very muddy sections. It's like discovering a person-sized model railway line in the forest and is great fun to run (or chug) along – but be careful not to slip.

When the river is very low, there are **several little beaches** along the route that are great for lazing on, digging holes or making castles.

The river here is famous for its fishing, and you may well see **fishermen** standing up to their waists in the cool water casting their lines. If you look carefully you may also see some very large fish coming to the surface to catch flies.

The Walk

Map OS Explorer OL5 The English Lakes (North-eastern area).

Refreshments In Kirkoswald you'll find two excellent pubs. The Crown, on the left as you go up the hill, is smaller and more intimate; the Fetherston Arms, on the right, has a large beer garden at the back.

1 From the parking area, take the stepped path up the bank through an area of clear felled trees. Cross the stile at the top and follow a faint track along the top of the riverbank cliff. There's a brilliant dead tree climbing opportunity here. The route follows the River Eden upstream and although the field is broad here, the bank to the right falls away steeply. You soon dip down towards river level, first crossing a plank bridge, then traversing a bog by way of the first of several boardwalks – this one a single plank's width. Continue past some gnarly old trees to reach a stile. Along the bottom of the next field you'll cross another little footbridge before reaching another stile. The Eden here is still and deep with fish breaking through the surface every now and then to snap insects out of the air. The next stile leads into a wooded area. Follow the narrow path over a series of little bridges before a final stile takes you into woodland proper.

2 Here you begin the magnificent boardwalk, transporting you over what used to be a succession of muddy dips and rises. The boardwalk snakes along the bank of the river, with occasional dry earth sections. Eventually it gives way to a sandy woodland path, still with the river drifting silently by to the right and woods climbing up the valley side to the left.

3 Emerging into a clear felled area you'll find a pleasant bench opposite a favourite reach for fishermen. At low water there's a good sandy beach here. Continue upstream and the character of the woods changes, adopting a more open appearance. As the path rises, take care with young children as the drop to your right steepens dramatically to form sandstone cliffs. The cliffs appear to your left as well, with one particular outcrop forming a shallow cave. It's only a hint of what is to come. Pass over a little bluff and down the other side. As you reach the bottom, turn sharp right, back on yourself beneath the cliff and you'll find yourself on a narrow ledge, passing between the crags.

4 A warning sign reminds you of the dangers. On your right a chamber has been hollowed out of the sandstone; beyond it several more can be found, connected by gloomy passages. The caves are quite safe (you don't really need a torch), though the drop from the 'windows' overlooking the river is precipitous. If you want to explore further, continue along the riverside path towards the waterfalls. In the woods you'll find the remains of an old plaster of Paris works as well as the sidings for the Long Meg gypsum mine. Take care though, as there are some unguarded drops here.

5 When you've finished exploring, return to the path and retrace your footsteps back downstream to Daleraven Bridge.

◆ Background Notes ◆

Lacy's Caves were built for Colonel Lacy of Salkeld Hall in the late 18th century. Lacy also attempted to demolish the famous Stone Age circle known as **Long Meg and her Daughters** (worth a visit after the walk). He sent his workmen to lay charges but, as they were about to commit this act of wanton archaeological vandalism, a storm blew up and the workmen fled, fearing they had upset the gods. The Long Meg site is just one of several ancient remains in the vicinity and finding them makes for an interesting tour on days when walking is a less attractive option. To get there from Daleraven, drive up Kirk Bank (there's a smaller stone circle in a private field to your left about halfway up) and continue through Glassonby, bearing right in the village. Follow the road round as it heads for Little Salkeld and you'll find Long Meg signposted up a lane on your right in about 3 miles (4.8 km).

The rock strata here was also very good for the formation of gypsum. Just beyond the caves you'll find the evocative remains of the **Long Meg gypsum mine**, once an important local employer and responsible for the removal of over 5 million tons of the mineral. Apart from a ghost of a siding off the Settle-to-Carlisle railway and a handful of tramway tracks in the woods, the only visible legacy is the subsiding road you are warned about as you ascend the bank to Glassonby from Daleraven Bridge. You pass along the base of this hillside at the start and finish of the walk. It's known as **Kirk Bank**, after a church that once served the lost village of Addingham. The Eden washed this ancient settlement away, perhaps even before the medieval period, but the replacement church can still be found, alone in a field beyond Glassonby. A story goes that you can hear the old church bell tolling from beneath the waters on dark, stormy nights.

Between the caves and the viaduct of the Settle-to-Carlisle railway the river flows over a natural weir. The water was harnessed to power not just the gypsum mine but a water mill on the opposite bank, which is now a picturesque, if somewhat noisy, holiday cottage, **Force Mill**.

Bitts and Rickerby Parks, Carlisle

In Search of the Roman Wall

Bitts Park playground

This walk starts beneath Carlisle Castle's massive eastern walls. The children may not notice this, however, because it also starts adjacent to the excellent play area in Bitts Park. Maybe a visit to the park should be left until the end – otherwise, especially on a hot day when the water feature is working, you may never get any further! The route follows a section of the Hadrian's Wall National Trail, though there isn't much Roman stuff to be seen. What you do get is a surprising slice of rural Cumbria, complete with grazing cows, poking right into the centre of the city. Following the River Eden in both directions you'll be surprised how quickly you leave the traffic behind, and as well as the obvious fun of the play area, there is the 'funny bridge' and the massive Rickerby Park monument to explore.

Getting there *There's a pay-and-display car park at Bitts Park, accessed off the eastbound lane of the Castle Way dual carriageway (the A595) in the centre of Carlisle. Approaching from the east, either head all the way up to the next roundabout and come back, or turn right, off Castle Way into West Tower Street. The park is back under the bridge behind you so you will have to find somewhere to turn round, taking the first turning on the left as you approach the slip road.*

Length of walk 2½ miles (4 km).
Time 1½ hours.
Terrain Riverside parkland. Suitable for all-terrain pushchairs.
Start/Parking Bitts Park car park (GR: NY398562). Toilets by the tennis courts.
Map OS Explorer 315 Carlisle.
Refreshments There is a kiosk in Bitts Park selling snacks and hot drinks and a café at the Sands Centre serving more substantial meals. Carlisle city centre is about 400 yards away.

◆ Fun Things to See and Do ◆

Bitts Park is a really exciting place. Apart from the brilliant play area, there's a maze and a Japanese garden to explore, and even a tiny race track, with miniature racing cars to be driven.

You're surrounded by history here, some more recent, some very ancient. Can you spot any remains of the **Roman wall**? The most you're likely to see are little waymarkers on the Hadrian's Wall Path. Look too for the massive **war memorial in Rickerby Park**. It seems a little odd, surrounded by fields with cows! The '**funny bridge**' is a suspension bridge connecting the city to the war memorial in the park across the river.

Close by, the **castle** is definitely worth exploring, and if you have time, go through the tunnel, past the 'Cursing Stone', to the **Tullie House Museum** where you can learn a lot more about this border city's fascinating history.

Bitts and Rickerby Parks, Carlisle

The Walk

① From the car park by the little cottage, walk into the park, towards the river, with the statue of Victoria on the right and the tennis courts and play area to the left. At a T-junction turn right and follow the broad path to meet the embankment of Eden Bridge. Go through the tunnel, emerging on the far side next to the Sands Centre. Look for the cormorant sculpture here, then keep ahead.

② Take a flight of steps down to the left. Imagine how much water it took to flood this space (see 'Background Notes'). Walk along the paved path for 100 or so paces before joining a grassy path alongside The Swifts golf course. If the river is low there are several little beaches down to the left here. Keep with the Hadrian's Wall Path markers between the willows, Himalayan balsam and giant hogweed. The pyramidal floodlights at Carlisle United's Brunton Park ground come into view as the path continues, now as a dual-use track with cyclists. As the river bends again, you'll see the metal bridge ahead.

③ Turn left over the bridge and on the far side choose the middle path, leaving the Hadrian's Wall Path, up an avenue of trees. At the war memorial, bear left on a narrower path across the meadow, touching the riverbank again by a car park.

4 Keep left now, on the riverside path, to a green gate. Go through this and continue downstream for ¼ mile (400 m) to a shallow weir. Now pick out a path going right, across the meadow to reach a higher path on the far side. It leads through an ornate gate into Eden Bridge Gardens, a more formal space, recently restored.

5 On the far side of the garden go up the steps to the busy main road. Turn left along the pavement across Eden Bridge. On the far side turn left down the ramp by the Sands Centre, and left again back through the underpass into Bitts Park. Now retrace your footsteps back to the car park.

◆ Background Notes ◆

Bitts Park and Rickerby Park are flood plains for the River Eden, Cumbria's longest river. It rises in the high hills on the Yorkshire border before flowing for 90 miles (145 km), finally making the sea at the Solway Firth, just a few miles north of Carlisle on the Scottish border.

The outward leg of this walk follows the **Hadrian's Wall Path**. There isn't much to see of the Roman wall in this part of Carlisle – it crossed the Eden at the northern end of Bitts Park, swinging north-east on the Stanwix bank between Linstock and Houghton. To the west it ran round the back of the Cumberland Infirmary.

The **castle** has its foundations on a Roman fort and was remodelled in massive stone in the 12th century. It has passed between England and Scotland a few times and saw action as late as 1745 in the Jacobite rebellion.

Tullie House Museum is free to enter for children and is one of Cumbria's best. As well as interactive exhibits on the Romans, the Border Reivers and the history of Carlisle, there is a fascinating section on natural history and an art gallery.